HUMAN NATURE
IN AMERICAN
HISTORICAL THOUGHT

HUMAN NATURE

IN AMERICAN

HISTORICAL THOUGHT

MERLE CURTI

The Paul Anthony Brick Lectures

Seventh Series

University of Missouri Press • *Columbia*

Standard Book Number 8262-7915-5

Library of Congress Card Number 68-29167

Printed in the United States of America

Preface

HAVING FOR MANY YEARS been interested in
ideas about human nature in American intellectual history, I welcomed the opportunity the
invitation to give the Paul Anthony Brick Lectures
provided for reporting some of my findings and reflections about this theme. Despite the fact that most
historians probably share the conviction expressed by
a doctoral candidate that she had no theory with
which to explain the behavior of the men she dealt
with in her dissertation, I have felt that historians
actually have been influenced by some theory of
human nature. This little book, consisting of the lectures I gave at the University of Missouri in the spring
of 1968, substantiates, I believe, my conviction. In

greater or lesser degree the writings of the historians chosen for analysis reflect one or another image of man and thus, on analysis, contribute to the understanding of the reputation of human nature in American thought. This inquiry also indicates that quasi-philosophical views, more or less optimistic or pessimistic, as well as common-sense views about human nature, have often informed the judgments and interpretations of historians. The third lecture indicates a trend toward the use of scientific concepts and tools that an increasing number of historians in our time have thought to be relevant to an understanding of human behavior in the past. If their implicit and explicit assumptions about human nature seem, in contrast with attitudes formerly expressed, to be amoral in giving little or no support either to an emphasis on man's limitations or on his potentialities under "favorable circumstances," these recent positions nevertheless suggest that knowledge of a precise and verifiable sort also has its own moral and ethical implications.

My notes can only inadequately express my indebtedness to a rich body of scholarship relevant to the subject that, nevertheless, has not been hitherto systematically explored over a considerable period of time. I want also to express my appreciation for the help several research assistants have given over the many years during which I have studied the changing reputation of human nature in American thought. These include Professor Richard S. Kirkendall, now a member of the History Department of the University of Missouri. I am indebted above all others to William R. Tillman, my research assistant during the academic year 1967–1968. I also want to thank my colleague Professor Max Savelle for his careful reading of the manuscript.

I am grateful to the Brick Lecture Committee and especially to its chairman, Professor William Peden, for many kindnesses and for the hospitality that made my visit to the University of Missouri one of the most delightful experiences I have had.

MERLE CURTI
Frederick Jackson Turner Professor of History
The University of Wisconsin

Madison, Wisconsin
March, 1968

Contents

I

THE LIMITATIONS OF MAN'S CAPACITIES

THE TERM *human nature* is still met with in everyday speech, though it appears less often than formerly in scholarly discourse. An exploration of its current meanings might well begin with biology, psychology, and anthropology. No one can belittle the knowledge these disciplines have given us about all normal human beings everywhere and about the qualities that relate men to and separate them from their nearest kinsmen in the animal world. If inquiry were to focus on the changing reputation of human nature, one might rather turn to literature and philosophy. These branches of learning have provided rich insights into motives, aspirations, and conflicts, into sufferings and defeats, into the capacity for understanding, for achievement, or at least for sustaining existence. History, whether original record or the writing of historians, might seem a less inviting path than the behavioral sciences, philosophy, or literature for these explorations, yet accounts of men's activities in the past offer a fruitful approach to what men have thought about human nature.

To be sure, few historians have made special studies of what has been thought about human nature in any period—Wilhelm Dilthey and Arthur O. Lovejoy are exceptions.[1] Although the larger theme is still in the main unexplored, other historians of thought have necessarily, if casually, referred to the varying images of man. A few historical essays have surveyed the changing reputation of human nature. The most important is the brief essay that John Dewey wrote more than four decades ago for the *Encyclopedia of the Social Sciences*.[2]

Dewey showed that the term *human nature* has been used in Western thought in a variety of ways, and he noted the correspondence between these meanings and the prevailing institutional and cultural character of the time. Only in the last century has the idea been explored with an effort at scientific objectivity. Dewey isolated four main ways of looking at human nature, from that of the Greeks to the view that is basic to contemporary scientific investigation of human behavior.

The first way designated an alleged original constitution—the innate equipment all men are born with as opposed to what is acquired through the experience of living. Aristotle's classic formulation of this view was a persisting influence. He held that, while some men are born with superior powers of reason, the great majority are so poorly endowed in this respect as to be inevitably dominated by the passions that make them, "by nature," slaves. Later, the Stoics modified this view of inborn and fixed capacities. These cosmopolitan philosophers of the Roman Empire taught, rather, that all men are equal in nature and that differences of status stem from convention, political organization, and economic relationships. In accepting this view, the early Christians, like the Stoics, rejected its revolutionary implications. In time these inferences were used to implement rising desires and to wage battle with existing authorities.

A second view defined human nature in terms of alleged psychological powers or faculties. These included perception, memory, judgment, and desire. These powers or faculties were assumed to be entirely separate from physical nature and from social life. This dualistic view expressed itself in a variety of forms. In the Hellenistic period, under the influence of Oriental religions and social disintegration, interest centered in securing favorable relationships with the supernatural. In adopting this view, Christianity deprecated nature in both its physical and social aspects and made redemption of the soul all-important. In the later medieval revival of Aristotelianism, nature, including the human body, became once again important, though, to be sure, still subordinate to soul or spirit. A turning point in the long and complex history of this dualistic view of human nature was reached when interest in and respect for nature became fashionable in early modern thought. John Locke found in the naturalistic structure of human nature the basis for natural law and natural rights. These he contrasted with an order of artificial civil and political rights that varied with conditions. This view was, among other things, related to the rise of the middle classes and to their challenge of traditional authority.

The third view of human nature assumed that human nature itself is empty and formless, capable of being molded by external circumstances. This theory, associated with Locke, was pushed further by his French successors, who logically made education and environment potentially all-powerful. A fourth theory held that human nature cannot be defined in terms of the constitution and characteristics of the individual, whether viewed as innate or acquired. Rather, human nature can be identified only through its great institutional products—language, religion, law, the state, and the arts. Any individual has merely the potentiality for the development of human nature, and this development can take place only under and through the influence of cultural institutions. Through most of its history this idea, suggested by Aristotle and developed by Hegel, was, in Dewey's account, a mere snapshot view of man at a given point in time, without much reference to biological or cultural change.

These four views were combined in many ways and according to many factors, among which the social needs of dominant and challenging groups of men seemed to Dewey to be of prime importance. In their main outlines, all four were accessible to the first as well as to the later Americans. Granting for the moment the acceptability of Dewey's analysis, we might expect Americans to combine these views of human nature in a variety of ways suitable to their condition, needs, and aspirations.

In contrast with philosophers, theologians, and psychologists, historians have rarely subscribed to well-defined theories about the nature of man—Thucydides and, in our own time, Toynbee are exceptions to the rule. Most historians have been preoccupied with concrete, unique data. At the same time, all historians, in interpreting the records, have made certain assumptions about human nature. From the time of the Greeks, those recounting the past have assumed that men act as they do because of their special relations to the gods, to the physical setting in which they live, and to their own natural endowments and limitations. Often these assumptions were implicit rather than explicit.

Several questions present themselves. Were the views of human nature that were expressed—or more often implied—superimposed by mere borrowing from theories available or popular at the time? Or were these derived from the study of man's behavior in time and place? To what extent did given theories about human nature really inform a historical narrative or explanation? Does one find, over time, changing views about or varying implicit attitudes toward human nature? If there is a recent concern among some historians with formal theories of human nature in contrast with traditional common-sense views, is this concern to be partly explained by the great crises in our time? Finally, what is the importance of this whole inquiry, both for a better understanding of historical scholarship as it has developed and for the reputation of human nature in American thought?

My hypotheses may be simply put. If the assumptions historians have made about human nature have been derived from the ideas about man's nature that were common to the period in which the historian lived, one might expect the largely unconscious choice of one view from among those at hand to be related to the historian's status at birth, his upbringing, and the social roles assigned to or chosen by him. The choice might also be influenced by the historian's temperament or personality, his optimism or his pessimism, his idealism or his sense of practicality. Also, of course, his opportunities for gathering information and for observing the behavior of his contemporaries might be expected to play a part in his view of human nature.

The history of ideas in America cannot be disentangled from the great movements of thought in Western civilization. Yet it may be assumed that American historians, writing about the national past, have reflected not only the ideas common to Western civilization at a given time but also those related to the distinctively American experience. While Dewey's classification of the main views about human nature in Western thought is relevant to American historians, it is not entirely adequate. A possible supplementary factor is the sensitiveness of these historians to the characteristic American environment, social structure, and emerging ideology. Without ignoring Dewey's scheme I have, in order to bring this factor into our cognizance, organized my findings under three main classes: historians whose view of human nature stressed man's limited capacities, those who on the whole reflected confidence in man's potentialities *under favorable conditions*, and those who sought guidance from scientific methods and theories.

Of the historians emphasizing man's limitations, the Puritans came first in time. The thought of these historians cannot be understood apart from the Puritans' general view of man. So, at the risk of treading too familiar ground, let me sum up the Puritan conception of human nature.

Until Descartes and Locke forced a revision of accepted views, New England's intellectual leaders generally subscribed to the medieval synthesis of the nature of human nature. One can say, while pleading guilty of oversimplification, that this view fused Aristotelianism and, in lesser degree, Platonic and Stoic conceptions with those of Judaeo-Christian theology. In this synthesis, as in Aristotle, the soul is composed of faculties, reason being the king and will the queen. Ideally, as in Stoicism, the two faculties served to make the soul intelligent and responsible by subordinating the passions and the emotions; in fact, this equilibrium did not operate, for in Adam's fall, we sinned all.

In accepting this over-all Thomistic psychology, the New England Puritans had to fit into it their peculiar ideas about grace and redemption—the federal theology that Perry Miller has expounded. The great mass of humanity, condemned to eternal damnation, would permit their baser passions to lead them astray again and again. But even the masses retained enough of reason to glimpse—however faintly—the image of the glorious and rational nature of God and His universe. The elect, blessed by grace, visioned this in clearer and firmer outlines. And the elect, like Plato's philosopher kings, were to help the less fortunate in gaining some part of that vision through knowledge and reason and the use of the emotions or religious affections to that end. The social controls that the rulers wisely and justly directed were additional instruments of guidance for the masses. From one angle of vision, human nature in this scheme is immutable, for God is sovereign and His plan, which is perfect, cannot be altered. But from another angle, human nature may be viewed as somewhat plastic, for hadn't God in His mercy and wisdom sifted a whole nation for seed to plant a new Zion in the wilderness? Here, thanks to His grace, the best potentialities of human nature were to be striven for under relatively favorable conditions. And, pervading and immutable though man's limitations were, it was hoped that these better potentialities might in part be realized.

This conception of human nature included some components of the four views outlined in John Dewey's historical scheme; it was the underlying assumption of the most enduring of New England's early historians —William Bradford, who started his *History of Plymouth Plantation* in 1630; John Winthrop, whose journal, begun in the same year, has come to us as *The History of New England;* and Cotton Mather, whose *Magnalia* was completed in 1701. I shall comment chiefly on Bradford.

The essential weaknesses of man were again and again explicitly stated by Plymouth's leader, whether he applied this idea in discussions of such fifth-columnists as Lyford and Oldham, of such a Judas as Isaac Allerton, of such a troublemaker—and in the end murderer—as John Billington, or in his generalized statements about the Plymouth community as a whole. Bradford also saw the proneness to sin in man's social and economic relations with his fellows as well as in the internal life. Yet Bradford did not go as far as Winthrop in making the sinfulness of farmers, laborers, and servants the justification for a governing elite. In relating the decision to replace Roger Williams as a "teacher" at Plymouth, he did not associate social and theological deviation with the Devil, as Winthrop and Mather did in recounting the banishment of dissenters from Massachusetts Bay.

In Bradford's view it is the beast in man that explains waves of sex crimes. These he discussed with a frankness that makes current novels and psychoanalytical case histories seem almost modest. "Marvilous it may be," Bradford wrote, "to see and consider how some kind of wickednes did grow and breake forth here, in a land wher the same was so much witnesed against, and so narrowly looked unto, and severly punished when it was knowne; as in no place more, or so much, that I have known or heard of." He laid this wickedness in the largest part to "our corrupte natures, which are so hardly bridled, subdued, and mortified." In explaining what appeared to be the excessive deviations of Plymouth, Bradford thought it possible that the Devil carried "a greater spite against the churches of Christ and the gospell hear." For Satan might have more power over even God's servants in lands long possessed by heathens like the Indians.

But another reason for the prevalence of such crimes was "that it may be in this case as it is with waters when their streames are stopped or dammed up, when they gett passage they flow with more violence, and make more noys and disturbance, then when they are suffered to rune quietly in their owne chanels. So wikednes being here more stopped by strict laws, and the same more nerly looked unto, so as it cannot rune in a comone road of liberty as it would, and is inclined, it searches every wher, and at last breaks out wher it getts vente."[3] This theory of repression would be treated with respect by contemporary psychologists. In the view of Bradford, as in that of Winthrop and Mather, a Christian society must base its sexual mores and laws, not on "the natural man," but on man in a state of grace. In other words, the norm rests, not on observed behavior, but rather on an abstraction that in turn rests on Christian revelation and faith. The heroic standard thus becomes the minimum, breaches of which are duly punished according to God's law.

However weak and sinful, man is capable in some part of understanding God's special providences as well as His larger plan. Bradford informed his own actions with reason, whether he was narrating what he and the chief men in the council did in the early struggle for survival, or was telling the story of how, in recognition of proper economic motives in behavior, the communal way was given up for individual responsibility in planting and harvesting, or was explaining what was done to resist the greedy attempts to nullify the patent, or was relating the imperialistic machinations of the Massachusetts Bay people. And Bradford also assumed a capacity of the rank and file to reason. That he wrote his *History* in the hope it might bring a new generation back to the pious example of the founders indicates some faith in man's reason. When his authority and policies were challenged, he reviewed in town meeting the story of the colony and appealed to reason as well as to sentiment for a vindication of what he had done. Similar examples of the role attributed to reason could be cited from the histories of Winthrop and Cotton Mather.

Bradford recognized individual differences in men, in addition to those that set the elect apart from the unregenerate. In justifying the abandonment of the communal experiment, he made the case in his often quoted, picturesque way. "Upon the poynte all being to have alike, and all to doe alike, they thought themselves in the like condition, and one as good as another; and so, if it did not cut off those relations that God hath set amongst men, yet it did at least much diminish and take of the mutuall respects that should be preserved amongst them." Mather's treatment of individual differences and his handling of the relation of innate to learned aptitudes are more sophisticated but not really different from Bradford's view. The

Plymouth historian implied that the superior abilities of some men laid on them the burden of stewardship for the less gifted. In the *History* this view suggests contemporary discussions of the father image: the leaders provided guidance and discipline as well as affection and security. Bradford again and again stated that human behavior can, through the covenant, bind men together in a blessed community dedicated to the Christian life. With no trace of the democratic overtones implicit in Bradford's view, Winthrop and Mather held to a similar concept of stewardship.

The Pilgrim historian believed in the innate inferiority of the Indian, as did Winthrop and Mather. He assumed that shrewd diplomacy, kind and fair treatment, might in general keep the Indians within bounds. But when these failed, God's elect could but "exerciese force . . . to reduse the Narigansets and their confederats to a more just and sober temper."[4] At the time of the Pequot war Bradford took an Old Testament delight in the colonists' triumph over the enemy, a triumph that betokened the operation of divine law and that was clearly predestined. In brief, when the Indians resisted the whites' advances, it was plain that their perfidiousness and treachery were both an innate failing and the work of the Devil.

With all the emphasis on fixed characteristics, with all the stress on viewing behavior and history as the unfolding of God's design, it might seem that the Puritans found no place for the idea that human nature can change. In a sense this is true, but it is only one side of the coin. Except for the minority who experienced regeneration, human nature was thought of as embracing a perpetually tumultuous conflict between the beast and the man. One is reminded of the Dionysian struggle between the vital will and the cognitive elements in the view of human nature depicted in the Greek tragedies. For the Puritan, even one who had received grace was not exempt from the temptations of natural man. More to the point, Bradford, in speaking of the decision to leave Holland, attached importance to environment. Recall his fear that the Puritans' offspring would be in danger "to degenerate and be corrupted" because of the "great licentiousnes of youth in that countrie, and the manifold temptations of the place."[5] America, on the other hand, appealed because "being devoyd of all civill inhabitants" it provided a condition where the faithful could build a commonwealth in which Christian law and piety would encourage the best of which man was capable. And in speaking of Plymouth's leadership, Bradford appreciated the point that the New World gave plain and untutored men a chance to discover their native talents for statesmanship, talents that must have lain dormant in the Old World. Furthermore, Bradford's emphasis on the scope the New World gave to the covenant by which men entered into sacred agreement for the individual and common good, suggests his belief that, if the American experience did not change human nature, it favored the most worthy expression of it. Even when prosperity came, when the colony dispersed into outlying areas, Bradford hoped that, by reminding the new generation of the sacrifices of the founders, some part of their special quality might be preserved in the time to come. If the New World provided conditions under which human nature might best exercise its talents of reason, will, and the governance of the beast in human kind, men nevertheless remained limited creatures, destined to act out a historical drama whose script they had no part in writing and whose roles were prescribed by what, in the over-all sense, was an immutable human nature.

It is a big stride from Bradford's *History of Plymouth Plantation* to the publication in 1764 of the first volume of Thomas Hutchinson's *History of the Colony of Massachusetts*. Of old New England stock, Hutchinson was a successful merchant, a learned lawyer, a member of the Massachusetts assembly and council, chief justice, and royal governor. The *History* reflects a concept of human nature both secular and Christian in character, one that regarded men as having fixed and unequal characteristics. This view was widely accepted by intellectual Americans in the later eighteenth century, especially by those New Englanders whom we associate with Arminianism, Old Light Calvinism, and the ingredients of what in time was to become the Federalist party.

Hutchinson's idea of human nature can be called "Christian" because it is static and because it combines other characteristics of Christian thinking about the nature of man: man has a spiritual as well as a physical nature (dualism), he is depraved by nature, and his depravity expresses itself in his pride. Hutchinson's historical judgments and interpretations reflect each of these ideas at one or another point.

That he believed in the spiritual component of man's nature is illustrated in his account of the witch trials of the 1690's.[6] The issue for him was whether witches actually exist or, in other words, whether there are evil spirits. Although Hutchinson did not believe in evil spirits, his cautiousness in dealing with this theme indicates his sensitivity to the implications of this belief for the existence of "good spirits." Throughout his discussion of the trials he offered rational explanations for each reportedly supernatural event, without insisting on his explanations. When he finally was forced to make a statement denying the existence of evil spirits, he very carefully cited legal opinions and even acts of Parliament. Although this refusal to scoff at witchery may arise in part out of a consideration for his New England audience and thus may not indicate a lingering superstitiousness in Hutchinson's thinking, it could hardly have come from a man completely committed to a naturalistic or "materialistic" image of man.

Hutchinson's adherence to the Christian idea of

natural depravity and to pride as man's chief sin is also illustrated in his discussion of the witch trials. Toward the end of his account, he attributed the causes of the episode to "the reluctance in human nature to reject errors once imbibed." Clearly, he had in mind pride, even though he did not use the word. He observed, "A little attention must force conviction that the whole was a scene of fraud and imposture, began by young girls, who at first perhaps thought of nothing more than being pitied and indulged, and continued by adult persons, who were afraid of being accused themselves. The one and the other, rather than confess their fraud, suffered the lives of so many innocents to be taken away, through the credulity of judges and juries."[7] The implication of this passage is that, while human nature might not in any sense be changed, men might control its inevitable tendencies by a shrewder application of the law.

While Hutchinson's view of human nature is "Christian" in the sense thus indicated, it must not be confused with more extreme versions of the same beliefs. His rationalistic Christianity had little in common with the Calvinism of William Bradford. The way in which Hutchinson dealt with the question of the existence of witches, by citing legal rather than biblical authority, shows how far his convictions differed from a strict adherence to revelation and traditional faith. Even more illustrative of the difference between Hutchinson and his Calvinistic predecessors is his treatment of the Antinomian controversy of the 1630's. After condemning his ancestress Anne Hutchinson as an "enthusiast," in which opinion Jonathan Edwards might have concurred, Hutchinson went on to betray a lack of sympathy not only with her but with most of what early New England stood for. With both bewilderment and disdain, he wrote, "She had, no doubt, some fine spun distinctions, too commonly made use of in theological controversies, to serve as a subterfuge, if there be occasion; and perhaps, as many other enthusiasts have done, she considered herself divinely commissioned for some great purpose, to obtain which, she might think those windings, subtleties and insinuations lawful, which will hardly consist with the rules of morality. No wonder she was immoderately vain, when she found magistrates and ministers embracing the novelties advanced by her."[8] The antimetaphysical bias in these comments places Hutchinson in a middle-of-the-road group theologically, one perhaps best exemplified by his contemporary, President Ezra Stiles of Yale.

It should be clear by now that Hutchinson had little to say, explicitly, about human nature; by temperament and personality, he was not theologically or philosophically but, in the main, legally and economically inclined. He made his career as a lawyer, administrator, and monetary theorist, and his interests are reflected in the questions he put to his sources. His whole analysis of the witchcraft episode, while his conclusion emphasizes the causal role of pride, focuses on the legal problems involved. This view is, of course, consistent with his feeling that, while human nature itself might not change, a shrewd application of the law might help control its manifestations. Similarly, Hutchinson gave considerable attention not only to the shortcomings of spectral evidence but to the inadequacies of the period's examination techniques as well. One instance of bad legal practice, that of a wife testifying against her husband, drew from him a sharp, and very rare, expression of personal revulsion: "Surely this instance ought not to have been suffered. I shudder while I am relating it."[9] Another striking example of the sorts of questions that preoccupied Hutchinson lies in his treatment of the 1740's. He devoted most of a long chapter to a discussion of the monetary policies of the Massachusetts government, with which he was deeply involved, yet failed even to mention the Great Awakening. Just as Hutchinson's discussion of legal practices might issue in a rare emotional reaction, so his discussion of the British Empire brought out his feelings about God: "The great creator of the universe in infinite wisdom has so formed the earth that different parts of it, from the soil, climate, &c. are adapted to different produce, and he so orders and disposes the genius, temper, numbers and other circumstances relative to the inhabitants as to render some employments peculiarly proper for one country, and others for another, and by this provision a mutual intercourse is kept up between the different parts of the globe."[10] It is as if Hutchinson's God thought more about the nature of trade patterns than about the nature of redemption.

Had Hutchinson been less engulfed in economics and in the more practical aspects of the law, had he been more the political theorist, or had he ever had to write a constitution, he might have developed his few notions about the relationship between law and human nature into a more elaborate exposition. The experiences of having to justify a revolution and to devise and justify a constitution seem, at any rate, to have drawn from another group of historians living in this same period a more direct and original view about man's nature. In the next lecture I shall consider this group of historians, a group that put more emphasis than Hutchinson on man's potentialities in a favorable setting. Let me now turn, however, to Francis Parkman, an outstanding representative of some of the main currents of thought in the mid-nineteenth century and, like Hutchinson, an exponent of the limitations of human nature.

The rational factor favored by some writers in the late eighteenth century was not entirely repudiated in the decades that followed. It was represented in the faculty psychology in academic circles, in the phrenological version of the old cliché that knowledge is power, and in the view that, in calculating his own interest and acting on it, the individual promotes the common good. But the dominant view in the middle nineteenth century stressed the limitations of man's rationality, the primacy of the will and the feelings, or what might be called the dynamic, voluntaristic and experiential aspects of human nature. To be sure, not all who emphasized the emotionality of human nature saw eye to eye. One emphasis within this general frame was on the power of sympathy, compassion, and voluntary association to right persisting social wrongs. But another and paradoxical emphasis was on the eternal inevitability of the tragic flaw in human nature, on an awareness of the sin of intellectual pride, and on the ravishing effects on body and mind of consciousness of guilt. Whatever the interpretation given to man's basic and overweening emotionality and the necessity of exerting will in inevitable conflicts, this image of man bore some relationship to the changes in the social structure wrought under the impact of an expanding frontier and the advance of industrialism. These historical experiences required a view of human nature that emphasized activity and the struggle for achievement, however adverse the situation.[11]

In narrating the titanic struggle of the French and British for colonial empire, Francis Parkman illustrated some of these mid-nineteenth-century emphases on man's limited nature.[12] A careful reading of his histories shows that he distinguished between a fundamental, inborn, and ubiquitous human nature and the diversities of character and behavior resulting from environmental experience. In his eyes the major driving impulses in the motivation and behavior of all men are hunger, thirst, self-preservation, sex, malice, envy, avarice, and an aggressive savagery. Each of these provided keys to innumerable historical explanations and interpretations. For example, in depicting Indian cruelty in blood-curdling images Parkman also reminded the reader of medieval sadism. In emphasizing the importance of bickerings over fur and in comparing these with the scramble for material gain in his own day, he concluded that "human nature has not changed since the birth of Adam."[13] With none of the reticence that marked the Victorian brand of romanticism, he stressed sex as one of the most important factors in explaining behavior. He regarded it as capable of expressing itself not only in the brutal exploitation of human beings, in a repression that was morbidly unwholesome, but also in ways that inspired man to noble action and esthetic creativity. Related to and overarching all these basic drives are man's aggressive, savage instincts, evident in his age-old fighting and cruelty.[14]

The American wilderness, the locale of Parkman's individual-centered and dramatic story, brought out man's basic weaknesses and such strengths as he might have. In the great forests the savagery of all human beings was given full and free play: man's aggressiveness, his proneness to exploit his fellowmen, and his capacity for brutality. At the same time the wilderness also evoked his capacity for physical endurance, hardship, and suffering, his ability—if he had what it took—heroically to triumph, at least for the moment, over great adversity. In a world that seemed to Parkman essentially disordered and irrational, such struggle against great odds in the raw wilderness might, then, enable some men, the true heroes, to transcend their natural limitations. Thus, Parkman made a hero of LaSalle, in actuality a half-crazed fanatic bent on triumphing over the great Mississippi River. William R. Taylor has suggested that in this interpretation Parkman was reflecting, in a compensatory way, his own inner conflicts and sense of inadequacy.[15] Parkman's glorification of masculinity and the strenuous life might also be regarded as a personal compensation for his illnesses, which seem to have been in part psychological.

Parkman's essays supplement the histories in his preoccupation with the limitations of human nature. The heroic greatness that sometimes resulted from struggles with the wilderness could not emerge in a non-evocative environment. Such heroism, Parkman felt, was not valued in civilized nineteenth-century America, with its materialism and its false egalitarianism. At the best, the proper kind of an education could restrain only some of the most undesirable traits of man that American culture accentuated. In holding that, though all men have the same inborn traits in their nature, these components are proportioned differently and result in more contrasts than resemblances among men,

Parkman opened the door to his belief in a natural elite and to the differences among races and nations. But overarching his racism, elitism, and antifeminism was his emphasis on the smallness and ineffectiveness of the human agency and the resulting essentially tragic view of human nature.

Parkman differed from most of his American predecessors and from his leading contemporary, George Bancroft, in not admitting divine intervention or even Providence as a factor in explaining man's activities in the past and, also, in his dislike of what he looked on as superstition and hypocrisy in institutionalized religion. Parkman's secular view of human nature as a factor in history was to become the hallmark of American historiography. A significant exception is Kenneth Scott Latourette, best known for his monumental history of the expansion of Christianity in modern times.[16] Another exception is Reinhold Niebuhr.

Although a theologian rather than a professional historian, Niebuhr has been a major figure in contemporary historical thought. His philosophy of history does, to be sure, subordinate his conception of human nature to his theology. Yet, implicit and often explicit in Niebuhr's philosophy of history is his image of man.[17] He drew on both the idealistic and "realistic" Christian versions of man's nature and, after rejecting his early religious and political liberalism, on Marxist theory, which he later repudiated. Niebuhr insisted that man is both a creature of history and a creator of it—a dual function that explains many of the ambiguities and ironies of history. This interpretation means that man is neither completely free nor completely bound, that he is neither the master of his fate, as much modern historical thought has assumed, nor yet the complete prisoner of his destiny. Man's social impulses, which relate him to other creatures in the animal world, are a source of both strength and weakness. But it is his untrustworthy rational gifts that have above all contributed to man's limitations—to his pride, self-esteem, and exaggerated sense of his capacity to manage both present and future. Men in their collectivities, that is, in racial, tribal, national, and class structures, have experienced more difficulties than man the individual in disciplining pride and in admitting self-interested behavior behind a veil of self-righteousness. Above all, men in such powerful aggregations as the United States have found it hard to assume the responsibilities of power without yielding to rationalized justifications of national policy. Thus, men, individually and collectively, have been thrust into tensions and conflicts between the paradoxes in their make-ups. These are, on the one hand, a rational endowment and a compassion that lead to expectations of a resolution of conflicts and, on the other hand, an innate and never-conquerable pride and egotism that make such a resolution impossible.[18]

Thanks to his theology and faith, Niebuhr found a way out of this predicament. He believed that God, sensing the human plight, would, at the end of history, resolve the conflict in man's favor by forgiving him for sins he could not avoid committing. As empirical evidence Niebuhr cited the human anxiety about death and about the end of history, man's ability to dream that which is not, to look both forward and backward, and his guilty sense of failure to fulfill God's absolute commands. Before the coming of the Kingdom at the end of human history, faith in Jesus the redeemer makes it possible for man to strive to improve the human condition without assuming, misleadingly, his own omnipotence and perfectibility on earth.

This conception of human nature, which Niebuhr developed in the 1930's, has, with some revisions, remained basically unchanged. It has informed his interpretation of the history of Western civilization and especially of the United States. In both *The Irony of American History* (1953) and in *A Nation So Conceived* (1963) written with Alan Heimert, it has played an important part in explaining the main problems in the American experience. These included the Federalist-Republican conflicts, the wars of expansion, the sense of an American mission, the Civil War, the paradox between professions of democracy and racial inequality and injustice, imperialism with its moral ambiguities and unconscious as well as conscious expression of lust for power concealed under a conviction of purity of motives, and the Cold War. Also included was the national character itself, which involved, as in the case of the individual personality, the search for identity and purpose. In Niebuhr's eyes the liberal image of man, oversimplistic, overrationalistic, and overconfident of man's power to correct evil, has led liberal historians to distort the national story. This distortion was evident in the unjustifiable overemphasis on the role of *laissez faire* and on the unrealistic effort to slough off the technical complexities of an industrial age by a return to an imagined earlier purity. The liberal version of American history also incorrectly pictured a conflict between idealism and intelligence on the one hand and pessimism and apathy on the other. Also inherent in the liberal version of the American story was the unwarrantable reliance on education and the social sciences as adequate techniques for solving the insoluble issues functional to man's limitations.[19] In *Man's Nature and Its Communities* (1963) Niebuhr argued that the first half century of American history refuted the liberal illusion that democracies are free of vice, despite national self-regard and ambition. Neither evangelical revivalism, with its stress on the ladder to heaven, nor democratic humanitarianism met the hard realities of slavery. Nor had the nation succeeded in accepting the responsibility of great power, with its corroding and poisonous attributes. Niebuhr's conception of human nature led him, however, to prefer, almost evangelistically, the "free nations" as against those committed to the inflexible ideology of Marxism.

In his later years Niebuhr broadened his early Augustinian and Lutheran conception of human nature by assimilating the social substance in the Jewish and Catholic traditions and some part of the behavioral sciences. His image of man continued, however, to identify human nature within a special cultural tradition. In this image he held to the conviction that man's spiritual need and expectation of ultimate salvation by divine intervention is an innate and unchangeable part of human nature. Niebuhr seemed unaware that the ancient Greeks and the Chinese, to cite two examples, lived with the problems of life and worked out ethical standards that guided conduct without reliance on faith in supernatural intervention for ultimate eternal existence. Moreover, Niebuhr's interpretation of history continued to rely less on empirical methods and proofs than on a highly abstract view of human nature and to reflect, in greater measure than he seemed to realize, an ideology. This basis for his interpretation is the more striking, in view of his hostility toward all other versions of human nature as bound by ideology.

Whatever the limitations of Niebuhr's view of man and of the uses he made of it in historical writing, he did offer a historical synthesis in which a common humanity, with all its limitations was, in perspective, not without deep and lasting meaning. It pointed to a nonspatial, nontemporal realm of eternity, or super-history, to which human history was subordinated and to which it led. "Perhaps," he wrote, "it is man's sorry fate, suffering from ills which have their source in the inadequacies of both human nature and human society, that the tools by which he eliminates the former should become the means of increasing the latter. That, at least, has been his fate up to the present hour; and it may be that there will be no salvation for the human spirit from the more and more painful burdens of social injustice until the ominous tendency in human history has resulted in perfect tragedy."[20]

That Niebuhr could hold out the possibility of this "perfect tragedy" being the deep and lasting meaning of history, distinguishes him from a group of secular historians, for the most part younger men coming to maturity in the late 1930's and early 1940's. It is debatable whether these "realists" were directly influenced by Niebuhr in their criticisms of the rosy and "innocent" picture of human nature held by the American people and their spokesmen until the eve of the Second World War and of the historians who, in accepting this concept, had allegedly given a misleading and even distorted interpretation of the American past. It is more likely that in considerable part these younger historians were reacting to the new and flagrant evidences of mass evil in totalitarianism and to the patent evidences of the complexities and confusions of their own time.

We can begin with Perry Miller, whose monumental

and erudite scholarship undermined many traditional views of the New England mind. Miller rarely offered in his historical writings any explicit statement about his own ideas on human nature or on any other subject, choosing rather to rely on irony and innuendo in presenting his ideas and thus making them all the more difficult to pin down. One comparatively explicit statement of his own viewpoint, however, was made in his introduction to *The Puritans*, written in the late 1930's. Drawing a contrast between the determinism of modern scientific thought and Puritan determinism, Miller observed that the chief difference lay in that "no matter how unintelligible the world might seem to the Puritan, he never lost confidence that ultimately it was directed by an intelligence." To modern scientists, on the other hand, history is determined by "blind forces." "Yet even with this momentous difference in our imagination of the controlling power," Miller continued, "the human problem today has more in common with the Puritan understanding of it than at any time for two centuries: how can man live by the lights of humanity in a universe that appears indifferent or even hostile to them? We are terribly aware once more, thanks to the revelation of psychologists and the events of recent political history, that men are not perfect or essentially good. The Puritan description of them, we have been reluctantly compelled to admit, is closer to what we have witnessed than the description given in Jeffersonian democracy or in transcendentalism. The Puritan accounted for these qualities by the theory of original sin; he took the story of the fall of man in the Garden of Eden for a scientific, historical explanation of these observable facts. The value of his literature today cannot lie for us in his explanation; if there is any, it must rest in the accuracy of its observations."[21] Thus, Miller's view of human nature was more or less compatible with that of Reinhold Niebuhr. The two differed in their answers to the problem their view of human nature implied: Niebuhr was willing to make a leap of faith; Miller gave no sign of being capable of such a leap.

One of Perry Miller's Harvard colleagues, Arthur M. Schlesinger, Jr., has been even more explicit in acknowledging the relevance of Niebuhr's view of man as a key to the utopian dreams and the assumptions of human innocence that have characterized so much American thinking and behavior. "The nineteenth century," Schlesinger wrote, "with its peace and prosperity, supplied protective coloration for the enthronement of history and for the rejection of the dark and subterranean forces in human nature."[22] To suppose that history teaches that "evil will be 'outmoded' by progress and that politics consequently does not impose on us the necessity for decision and for struggle" seemed to Schlesinger to be fully and uncritically exemplified by the revisionist historians of the Civil War. These saw in slavery a minor and waning phenomenon inflated from its natural proportion by emotional extremists North and South. Writing much as Niebuhr would have written, Schlesinger went on to claim that "history is not a redeemer, promising to solve all human problems in time; nor is man capable of transcending the limitations of his being. Man generally is entangled in insoluble problems; history is consequently a tragedy in which we are all involved, whose keynote is anxiety and frustration, not progress and fulfillment. Nothing exists in history to assure us that the great moral dilemmas can be resolved without pain; we cannot, therefore, be relieved from the duty of moral judgment on issues so appalling and inescapable as those involved in human slavery; nor can we be consoled by sentimental theories about the needlessness of the Civil War into regarding our own struggles against evil as equally needless."[23]

The rising view in historical interpretation that American progressivism rested on an unrealistic "soft and shallow" conception of human nature and was thus unable to explain or control the "tragic movements of history in the twentieth century" found early expression in Schlesinger's *Vital Center*. But a group of younger historians, including David Noble, Cushing Strout, and Louis Hartz, in more fully documented and finished writings, similarly indicted progressivism —and historians presumably under its influence—for a naive belief in progress and for thus drifting "along the smooth utopian routes they had imposed on the roughness, the contradictions, the problems of their America."[24] Historians of American foreign relations in somewhat the same vein held up to scorn the progressives as well as the people as a whole for their ignorance of "the real limits upon the efficacy of impulse and moral sentiment in international relations," an ignorance and innocence uppermost at least until the approach of the Second World War.[25]

But it was in intellectual history that the accent on an "innocent" picture of man's nature was most fully expounded. Henry May's *The End of American Innocence* (1959) argued that between the late nineteenth century and the end of the First World War a cultural revolution undermined the Victorian and progressive optimism about the possibility of progress and a simplistic acceptance of an absolute morality. In the place of the traditional view of man and society, a more sophisticated view, which May characterized as "beyond innocence," largely took over. This of course emphasized the limitations of rationality, malleability, and goodness in man's make-up and of the related "realistic" view of history, society, and the course ahead.[26] The general theme of "innocence," with special reference to the picture of man, was further developed by R. W. B. Lewis in *The American Adam: Innocence, Tragedy, and Tradition in the Nineteenth Century* (1955). Lewis, like May, held that the traditional view of the American as an innocent Adam in the Garden had been replaced in "the age of containment" by one that was sensitive to new psychological, political, and social realities and insights and that was "more clearly warranted by public and private experience in our time."[27]

In the next lecture I shall present another view of human nature, that which stressed the moral potential of man. Perhaps we may then better assess the criticisms made of this view and of the historians who allegedly permitted it to inform what they wrote.

II

EMPHASIS ON MAN'S POTENTIALITIES

WITH LITTLE DISSENT scholars now agree that eighteenth-century intellectual life was too pluralistic to be seen as an overarching revolt against Christian piety and doctrine. Nor was it dominated by a belief in man's ability, through reason and science, to shape his own destiny. In the religious sphere eighteenth-century thought and feeling embraced pietism and evangelism as well as Arminianism and deism. A secular emphasis on man's innate emotional nature included an ineluctable endowment of pride, self-esteem, and emulation. These seemed to restrict human freedom hardly less than the Christian doctrine of innate depravity. At the same time a cluster of ideas, often diverse and even contradictory, may be thought of as the Enlightenment. Broadly speaking, the Enlightenment repudiated the orthodox views of a sovereign and arbitrary Creator and a necessarily frail if not helpless human creature. For this earlier creed the Enlightenment substituted ideas familiar to the pagan philosophers of antiquity, reliance on reason and on the science of the new age, belief in progress, the malleability of human endowments, the important roles of environment and education, and the possibility of freedom and happiness in this world.

It seems likely that only a minority of eighteenth-century Americans accepted all these ideas, even though many others were in some part influenced by them. But the Americans who did respond favorably included intellectual leaders whose attitudes were influential. Moreover, these did not respond merely in a passive or imitative way. The American Enlightenment has been characterized by one of its gifted interpreters as distinctive in more than one respect.[1] It democratized many of the humanistic values of the Age of Reason, including the idea of the dignity of man and the right of all men to take part in the making of decisions affecting the public weal. The American Enlightenment was also marked by an experimental and practical temper in the sphere of action as well as of thought, exemplified in the struggle for freedom and independence and in the creative acts of drafting self-governing constitutions and then in making them work.

The Americans who may be identified in some part with the Enlightenment include writers of history and of essays or treatises reflecting a conception of history. In all of these, ideas about human nature that reflected the values and thought of the Enlightenment, or some aspect of it, found expression.

We may begin our discussion with an American classic that, while not history in any formal sense, made use of historical materials and has served as a storehouse for historians ever since it was first published in Paris in 1785 in an effort to clarify and correct French views about America that were sometimes sentimental and sometimes critical. Jefferson's famous *Notes on Virginia* reflects his deep belief in the value of history. It also reflects the Enlightenment's penchant for an empirical approach to data and a critical handling of them. Moreover, it is programmatic in the sense that it was designed, as Jefferson believed all good historical writing should be designed, to teach men useful lessons about living together. Unlike the Puritan historians, Jefferson virtually ruled out the intervention of God as an explanation of historical events and human behavior. He frankly placed events involving human behavior within the sphere of nature. Thus, he devoted a large part of his book to a description of the topography, geology, and economy of Virginia. Jefferson believed that it is necessary to depict clearly and accurately the stage on which a human drama is being enacted. In Jefferson's time it was, in the case of Virginia and, by implication, of America itself, a stage so goodly that it could, and he believed would, promote the expression of man's better potentialities. In saying this he also made it clear that "human nature is the same on every side of the Atlantic, and will be alike influenced by the same causes."[2] After empirically refuting the assumption, widespread among prestigious European savants, that the physical environment in America stunts the stature of man and beast, Jefferson discussed the relation between environment and man's essential human traits.

Reason or intelligence is, of course, one of these. Influenced by such French materialists as Cabanis, Jefferson regarded thinking as "a mode of action" or "a particular organization of matter" rather than a supernatural instrument.[3] Intelligence, he easily granted, is unequally distributed, but he did not suppose that superior powers of reasoning and judgment are confined to the socially prominent and wealthy, as his plans for an educational system testify. To be sure, Jefferson, like the Puritan historians before him and like St. Paul before them, considered women as a group to be less intelligent than men. But whatever the inequalities in the distribution of intelligence, he felt that it is spread widely enough to enable the average man to share in making the decisions that affect him, provided he is properly enlightened by free schools and a free press.

In Jefferson's view all men, in all times and places,

are imbued not only with reason and an innate moral sense but also with a paradoxical impulse toward power and greed. Here he was, of course, reflecting not only a traditional Christian view of man's innate endowment but also a dominant conviction of most secular eighteenth-century thinkers. Thus, the great human problem is to use intelligence and the moral sense of men to restrain the lust for greed and power. The moral sense can find its fullest expression in a favorable environment. Such was the rural society of eighteenth-century America, in which the bulk of the population owned freehold farms that exempted them from constant temptation to subservience and corruption. Jefferson further felt that human nature includes a need for freedom and for the right to pursue happiness. "The sheep," he wrote, "are happier of themselves than under the care of the wolves." This statement points to a government strong enough to protect the sheep. Given the existence of innate impulses for power and greed, Jefferson emphasized the importance of "constant vigilance" on the part of the community toward its governors. Such vigilance can operate best, he felt, in the small community, in the state where truly representative institutions prevail. He further insisted that a system of checks and balances is necessary in a constitution, since there is in all those entrusted with government some trait of human weakness, some germ of corruption and degeneracy that cunning will discover and wickedness insensibly open, cultivate, and exploit.

Did Jefferson think that human nature can be changed? I have already noted that he believed it to be the same on both sides of the Atlantic and at all times to contain elements of weakness and of strength. But he thought that human traits—weakness, corruption, venality, the boisterous passions on the one hand and reasonableness, morality, and dignity on the other —are subject to the institution, the situation, and the general environment that form personality in infancy and childhood. A case in point was the unfortunate effect of slavery on character. Children, imitating adults as they do, from the very cradle learned to model their own behavior on the intemperance, passion, and tyranny that all too often marked the attitude of adults toward slaves. By the same token, the early impact of the monarchical environment in Europe on personality and character was so deeply ingrained that Jefferson doubted whether most immigrants could throw it off or, if they did, whether they would not exchange it for "an unbounded licentiousness, passing, as is usual, from one extreme to another."[4] But Jefferson's view of the role of environment also opened the possibility to considerable improvement in the expressions of human nature, that is, in behavior. As I have noted, he was convinced that the essential potentiality for goodness in men stands its best chance of being approximated in an open society of independent freeholders, "God's chosen people, if he ever had a chosen people." How long the abundant space and resources of America would permit this type of society to dominate was a question that concerned Jefferson, but some decisions relevant to the outcome could be made. These included the extent to which the American people would encourage or discourage the growth of cities and industries.

The Virginia statesman's view of the Negro has been much argued. He recognized that his own opportunities as an observer were limited to a slaveholding society. He recognized the difficulties in making any valid empirical judgments about such intangible factors as the Negro's capacity for abstract reasoning. Mental tests had not yet been invented! He also believed that some of the most marked examples of misbehavior, such as theft, could easily be explained in terms of poverty and slender ethical training. Jefferson saw no evidence that the Negro was lacking in imagination or in the qualities of the heart. He did, however, hesitantly and tentatively, express the view that the Negro is innately deficient in the powers of abstract reasoning. It was partly because of this lack that he questioned whether freedom would improve the Negro sufficiently to make him an acceptable neighbor on terms of equality.

Jefferson's conception of the limitations within which human nature could be changed is also evident in his comments on war. He believed that Americans, thanks to the generosity of natural resources, might, if they chose, avoid the ruthless jockeying for position and power that had led to so much bloodshed in the Old World. At the same time he recognized the American commitment to commerce, a commitment that in his view invited wars. But he believed it is possible to reduce the incidence of war by making the economy as self-sufficient as possible and by avoiding acts of injustice toward others. To this extent, at least, it is possible to redirect the kind of human impulses that had traditionally issued in war.

Jefferson hoped that a fellow citizen with these general views about the relation of the American scene to improvement in the expression of human nature would undertake a systematic history of America and, especially, of its late Revolution. He tried to persuade his friend and disciple Joel Barlow to embark on the task and generously supplied him with pertinent materials. But it was left for others, more or less sympathetic with the view about human nature in Enlightenment thought that he espoused, to try their hands at writing an American history imbued with his image of man.

Although sharing some of Jefferson's views of human nature, Dr. David Ramsay of South Carolina, a moderate Federalist politician as well as a disciple of the well-known physician Benjamin Rush, did not entirely accept, in his *Revolution in South Carolina* (1785) and in his *History of the American Revolution* (1789), the view of human nature as malleable and perfectible and as capable of directing destiny, which some of the Enlightenment men espoused. To be sure, Ramsay's histories reflect the idea of man as having rational powers. The important fact about man's rationality, in Ramsay's view, is that it enables him to understand the general will of Providence as presented in revelation, to experience the special will of Providence, and to conduct himself accordingly. Providence, Ramsay believed, has willed that men ought to be free, self-governing, and "equal in their right to life, liberty, property and happiness." Gifted with the power to experience American history and, especially, the American Revolution, a man might understand and move closer to Providence's plan for his freedom and happiness. This understanding could be achieved largely through the human power to experiment with political and social institutions and forms designed to enable him to realize the capacities with which Providence has endowed him.[5]

Without fully accepting the premises of Professor Arthur O. Lovejoy's analysis of eighteenth-century ideas about human nature, it is fruitful to apply one of his methods of analysis, as presented in *Reflections on Human Nature,* to Ramsay's *History of the American Revolution.* According to Lovejoy, eighteenth-century writers often confused, but in illuminating ways, one aspect of human nature with another aspect. They might, for example, distinguish between desire for approbation, self-esteem, and emulation, lumping all three of these characteristics under a single attribute, *pride* or *ambition*. Or they might confuse different manifestations of the same basic characteristic, the desire for approbation, for example, with entirely distinct aspects of man.[6] David Ramsay presented a revealing instance of this sort of confusion in his treatment of the motives of each side in the American Revolution. While he claimed that the British were motivated by a desire to make the Colonies "subservient to their avarice and ambition," he stated that the American patriots, in the larger sense activated by an emotional rather than a rational hatred of tyranny (insofar as they had rational goals), sought primarily "the prospect of honours and emoluments in administering the new government."[7] Actually, the Americans' desire for approbation in the form of "honours and emoluments" differs from the British "avarice and ambition" only in that it is American. Both are manifestations, in Lovejoy's terms, of precisely the same aspect of human nature: the desire for approbation.

By using these very different labels to describe the same aspect of human nature as manifested in different nationalities, Ramsay betrayed a crucial and characteristic bias. Throughout his *History,* he leaned toward the Jeffersonian idea that human nature somehow has greater potential in America than it has in Europe. The Americans, he maintained, have a natural "genius" for "republican habits and sentiments," which allows America to achieve politically and socially what Europe probably could never achieve.[8] Thus, American ambition lacks the evil connotations that adhere to European ambition because there is something in the American "genius" that allows ambitions to be fulfilled honestly.

A natural question for anyone concerned with Ramsay's idea of human nature is whether this American genius consists in less ambition or whether it consists in the greater possibility for fulfilling normal ambitions honestly. That Ramsay took the latter view is clear from his explanation of the sources of the American love for freedom. It is in the nature of man to love freedom, as I have noted, but there are certain conditions under which man's love of freedom can grow into passion. Thus, the "distance of America from Great Britain generated ideas in the minds of Colonists favourable to liberty," not because there were no seeds of the idea to begin with, but because, at the "extremities" of the Empire, the colonists grew more accustomed to the benefits of traditional English liberties than to their obligations. This was likewise true of their relationships with their own colonial governments: "The natural seat of freedom is among high mountains and pathless deserts, such as abound in the wilds of America."[9] Human nature, then, is fixed, but the American landscape draws out man's best potentialities.

Not only the American landscape but the American social structure helps to account for the growth of liberty: "The Colonies were communities of separate individuals, under no general influence, but that of their personal feelings and opinions. They were not led by powerful families, nor by great officers in church or state. Residing chiefly on lands of their own, and employed in the wholesome labours of the field, they were in great measure strangers to luxury. Their wants were few, and among the great bulk of the people, for the most part, supplied from their own grounds. Their enjoyments were neither far-fetched, nor dearly purchased, and were so moderate in their kind, as to leave both mind and body unimpaired. Inured from their early years to the toils of a country life, they dwelled in the midst of rural plenty. Unacquainted with ideal wants, they delighted in personal independence. Removed from the pressures of indigence, and the indulgence of affluence, their bodies were strong and their minds vigorous."[10] So, the American freeholding system of small, largely independent farms also contributed to the greater potential of human nature in America.

I must pass by Ramsay's acute analysis of the reasons why some Americans took the revolutionary, others the loyalist side. It would also be relevant to indicate how Ramsay's idea of human nature was used to explain why some Americans, subject to "the vices and follies of human nature," failed to see the need and merits of the Constitution even though they had—also in response to human self-interest—been spurred on to a spirited resistance to invasions of their rights. But those who were willing to surrender some part of their natural liberties under the restraints of a firm government so necessary to bridle the ferocity of man, proved the human capacity to act on a higher plane than immediate self-interest. Nor can I do more than refer to one of the most striking passages in Ramsay's history, in which he indicated that, while the Revolution had called forth great vices, it had also released great virtues and occasioned the display of abilities that otherwise would have been lost to the world. "While Americans," he wrote, "were guided by the leading strings of the mother country, they had no scope nor encouragement for exertion," but as they pursued their objects in the Revolution with ardor, "a vast expansion of the human mind speedily followed. It was found that their talents for great stations did not differ in kind, but only in degree, from those which are necessary for the proper discharge of the ordinary business of civil society." It seemed as if the war not only required but also created talents. Men whose minds were warmed with the love of liberty and whose abilities were improved by daily exercise and sharpened with a laudable ambition to serve their distressed country, spoke, wrote, and acted with an energy far surpassing all expectations that could be reasonably founded on their previous acquirements. To be sure, selfish passions began to operate after the war had been won. But even Ramsay's personal misfortunes, leading to bankruptcy, did not negate his faith that "the elasticity of the human mind, which is nurtured by free constitutions," kept and would keep the American people from falling prey to despondency. The record of human failures in the past and the challenges of the present, Ramsay concluded, provided the citizens of an independent America an opportunity to wipe off this aspersion, "to assert the dignity of human nature." The record might well stimulate the American people to sustain, continue, and extend the principal aims of the Revolution and thus aid them, under America's favorable circumstances, to realize many of man's potentialities and to transcend many of his limitations.[11]

To a much greater extent than Dr. Ramsay, Mercy Otis Warren, a versatile poet and playwright, an intimate associate of many of New England's Revolutionary patriots, and a correspondent of Jefferson, explicitly invoked human nature as a guiding interpretive principle in her lively and penetrating *Rise, Progress, and Termination of the American Revolution* (1805). Like Ramsay, she associated human freedom with Providence or divine will; like him, she believed that human nature is static and depraved, at least as it had manifested itself throughout most of man's history. The central principle of human nature, in the eyes of this strong-minded and democratic patriot, was ambition (man "pants for distinction"), and this ambition might and did turn to avarice "if a favorable coincidence of circumstances permits."[12] Looking back over man's long past, she argued that the high stages of civilization, such as ancient Rome and pre-Revolutionary England, provided especially favorable circumstances for the development of avariciousness. Further, in her opinion, the most primitive stages of society offered equally favorable "circumstances."[13] Man's only hope, Mrs. Warren contended, lay in that "just and happy medium" between, on the one hand, the "ferocity of a state of nature" and, on the other, the profligacy and luxury of refined civilization. This middle stage is characterized by the presence of piety, morality, hospitality, authority, justice, regularity, peace, and by its educated population.[14]

Mrs. Warren maintained that, with the passing of the religious bigotry of an earlier Massachusetts Bay, this "just and happy medium" had existed in America immediately before the Revolution. One may infer that the presence of this sort of society, in her opinion, helped to bring about the Revolution, which was in this sense an expulsion of evil from God's chosen country. The political implications of this historical view are evident in the Introduction to her book. Here she wrote, "Providence has clearly pointed out the duties of the present generation, particularly the paths which America ought to tread. The United States form a young republic, a confederacy which ought ever to be cemented by a union of interests and affection, under the influence of those principles which obtained their independence. These have indeed, at certain periods, appeared to be on the wane; but let them never be eradicated by the jarring interests of parties, jealousies of the sister states, or the ambitions of individuals."[15] It was thus with concern that she detected in the tensions between Republicans and Federalists threats to the will of Providence, to the high degree of rationality and morality she ascribed to the American people, and to the favorable circumstances their environment and experience offered. The caustic analyses of the opponents of the Revolution that she had included in her history were later directed against John Adams, who resented what he regarded as her unfair treatment in alleging his "pride of talents and much ambition." In the end a reconciliation was effected with an exchange of affectionate letters and even locks of hair, though privately Adams told the go-between, "History is not the province of ladies."[16]

We do not know whether Mercy Warren's wide circle of acquaintances included Samuel Williams,[17] Hollis Professor of Mathematics and Natural Philosophy at Harvard from 1780 to 1788 and author of a now almost unknown history that is important both in itself and by reason of its focus on human nature in relation to society and to nature. A liberal Congregational minister before assuming the Harvard professorship, Williams contributed to science with enough distinction to win him honorary doctorates from Yale and Edinburgh as well as the prestigious chair at his alma mater. In 1788, as the result of a scandal—financial, not amorous—he was dismissed from Harvard. He fled to Vermont, where he served as the local minister at Rutland, edited a newspaper and a periodical, surveyed disputed boundary lines, and helped found the University of Vermont. At the University he delivered in 1808 and 1809 a series of lectures. It is likely that these synthesized late eighteenth-century knowledge and ideas in science, social relations, and theology, for we have such a synthesis in a long manuscript in his hand. I discovered this manuscript many years ago, and it is still unpublished. We do have his *History of the American Revolution,* a popular reading book for schools, and his *Natural and Civil History of Vermont,* published in 1794 and again in 1809.

Williams' *History* is remarkable for a number of reasons. In its respect for the documents the author had collected before writing it and in its comprehensiveness and objectivity, it excels the much better known *History of New Hampshire* by the Reverend Jeremy Belknap. It recognizes the importance of America for world history and, like the histories of Mrs. Warren and David Ramsay, drives home the need to understand the distinctive character of America. The *History* is also the most important early example of the idea that the establishment of a new nation in an unexploited wilderness opened the possibility of implementing man's rational endowment in a rationally organized society, something that had been impossible in the Old World. In the Newtonian vein Williams held that men, at least under favorable circumstances, could understand and act on the natural laws that apply not only to the physical universe but to the political structure of societies as well.

Williams' assumption involved a conception of human nature that placed men squarely in nature and argued that their history, current situation, and future depend on their proper or improper relations to the nature of which they are a part. History has proved that, if men are to be truly free and if they are to realize their potentialities, they must properly relate themselves to nature. Thus, the Indian or, as he called him, the American Man, far from being the degraded beast that some European philosophers made him out to be, was actually a human being in rapport with nature.[18] Other examples of Williams' ecological theory of human nature in history are his depiction of the colonial movement from religious bigotry to toleration, the unfortunate effects on the Colonies of wars in which the Americans had no genuine stake, the Revolution, and what Williams called the *state of society*.[19] All these were in turn related to his view of human nature.

In sum, Williams held that the different peoples of

the human race resemble one another in the make and form of their bodies, in their original appetites, passions, and understandings, and in the potential moral sense. But in these respects nature has produced similitude, not equality. To some the Author of Nature has assigned superior powers of mind, a strength of reason and discernment, a capacity for judging, and a genius of invention not given to others. Superior wisdom and abilities exert superior influence in society. Men so endowed are thus gifted with a greater potential for social usefulness. Notwithstanding these innate differences, an equality of the rights of all men inheres in nature, even though throughout most of history the existing states of society have denied this equality and have thus thrust men into a distorted and false relationship with nature and nature's laws.[20]

Human nature, then, was for Williams a constant, subject to regular and uniform laws and to the state of society. The same state of society, anywhere and at any time, would produce the same forms of government, the same manners, customs, habits, and pursuits, whether monarchical or republican institutions, whether superstition or truth. States of society are the variables, human nature the constant.

With this frame of reference it was necessary for Williams in his history to describe in detail the topography, climate, economy, and society of Vermont. (In so doing, he took occasion to offer evidence, as Jefferson had, to refute the ideas of Buffon and other philosophers on the deteriorative effects of an alleged unfavorable physical environment on beast and man in the New World.)[21] But what was taking place in his new frontier home, the good balance between man and nature, had likewise been approximated with lasting results in the older sections during their formative period. Thus, initially, the colonists had no more knowledge of the rights of human nature than their neighbors in the Old World, as their religious intolerance and oligarchical hierarchy made evident. But the severe handicaps and suffering, necessary in adjusting to new conditions, did for the colonial Americans what reason had failed to do. Thus, the common folk came to a better understanding of the rights and privileges inherent in the natural order than was evinced by any European philosopher. To be sure, Williams recognized that the state of society changes and the human condition along with it. He did not see that the state of society in the older regions was indeed changing in a way that led some to be concerned for the future. At the same time Williams, like other late eighteenth-century men influenced by the Enlightenment, did reject the cyclical theory of historical change and stood for the idea of progress, at least for America. In any case, the Americans' achievements in molding the state of society, thanks to favorable circumstances, hardships, and the use of reason, provided guidelines for the future.[22] *The Natural and Civil History of Vermont*, more than any of

its contemporaries, interpreted the American experience in terms of man's improvability and thus anticipated the first great national historian, George Bancroft, and one of his most influential successors,
Frederick Jackson Turner.

The emphasis on man's potentialities under favorable circumstances, which informed so much of Bancroft's *History of the United States*, can best be understood in terms of the economic and social developments in the first decades of the nineteenth century
and of new movements in our intellectual history.
These, briefly, were the several romantic movements,
including Transcendentalism, that emphasized the importance of emotions, intuitions, and the will.[23]

George Bancroft differed from Parkman in finding
in man's historical experience the guiding hand of
God and in rejecting the tragic view of man's limited
human nature. To say this is not to say that Bancroft's
view of man was one of unlimited optimism or that
he accepted the dogma of man's perfectibility. His
critical judgments on several colonial figures illustrate
his conviction that human nature is a mixture of good
and bad and that, perhaps because of inherited "tem-
peraments," some men are destined to play historical
roles that are mainly harsh or unwise or both.[24] On
the other hand, Bancroft emphasized the idea that
all men, including the savage Indians, are endowed
by the Creator with reason—which for Bancroft included an intuitive capacity for reaching truth—with

a moral sense, and with a capacity for love. Since any one person might not realize all these capacities, Bancroft gave great weight to collective judgment and wisdom, that is, to democratic decision-making. Education, an imperative necessity for this son of a Unitarian minister, was bound to play an important part in helping men realize their better potentialities. So was the social environment. Intensely patriotic and nationalistic, Bancroft was convinced that the American scene is peculiarly fitted to bring out the best in man. It nourishes his innate desire for freedom; it provides opportunities for the full play of his better conscience; it develops his ability to invent, to reason, to understand, to take part in making decisions. Bancroft did not, to be sure, think that men are endowed with free will—his praise of Jonathan Edwards' philosophy is one index. But Bancroft's more comprehensive emphasis, derived from Transcendentalism, on the ability of everyone to approach the truth, informed his optimistic image of man within the frame of the American record and the national character.[25] The *History of the United States,* from the founding to the Constitution, bore witness to the conviction that every human being, above all every American, might in developing his natural endowments contribute to the improvement both of himself and of the society that favored such improvement.[26]

While Bancroft was touching up the final revision of his work, young Frederick Jackson Turner was beginning his in Wisconsin. In his historical thought Turner looked both backward and forward. Like Bancroft, he conceived of American history in nationalistic, democratic, and environmentalist terms, putting, of course, a distinctive emphasis on the role of abundant cheap lands in releasing social restraints and in encouraging such human potentialities as individual self-direction, self-confidence, and adaptability. On the other hand, Turner was the herald of a rising group of historians. With them he believed that, in spite of the inevitability of relativism in even the most objective scholarship, it is possible to make historical writing more scientific. Further, historical writing might also become an instrument for helping Americans to face grave problems.[27]

The formal launching in 1912 of the movement with which Turner had some kinship was related to the growing awareness of the industrial and urban dislocations in American life and to the associated progressive protest and program for social reconstruction. Also important in explaining the new emphasis in historical thought was the impact of psychology and especially of functional psychology. Briefly, its view of man, as developed by William James, James Rowland Angell, and John Dewey, in accepting the evolutionary theory of the unity of the human organism rejected the dualism of body and mind, thought and deed. Human behavior was largely explained as the organism's unending adjustment to its environment, in the process of which the environment was itself often changed. Thinking and ideas thus were regarded as the problem-solving functions of the organism, in the process of which trial and error, emotional equipment, and habit played important roles. This emphasis in the new experimental psychology on function, along with other factors, found a philosophical counterpart in pragmatism and instrumentalism. Moreover, it was an important factor in shifting the traditional emphasis in the social sciences from formalistic, a priori, abstract, and absolutistic "laws" to an empirical and relativistic emphasis with a programmatic promise of social control in the direction of minimizing social evil and maximizing social good. It was almost inevitable that all these developments, the social situation, the progressive movement, and the new emphasis in psychology, philosophy, and the social sciences should find expression in historical thought. It is of course also true that the "new history" was in one or another way anticipated by certain eighteenth-century philosophers, notably Voltaire, and by such nineteenth-century figures as Henry Thomas Buckle, Hippolyte Taine, Auguste Comte, Frank Lester Ward, the founder of American sociology, Richard Ely, who linked economic science with social reform, and Edward Eggleston, an American pioneer in social and cultural history who sought to broaden the content of historical writing and to focus greater attention on the role of superstition and social habits in historical experience.

The leading spokesman of the "new history" was, of course, James Harvey Robinson of Columbia, whose early scholarship had been traditional in its emphasis on political and institutional developments, the careful exploitation of a limited number of primary sources, and the conviction that historical study was in the main properly devoid of implications and lessons, at least in a presentist and programmatic sense.[28]

The leaders of the new history, James Harvey Robinson, Charles A. Beard, Carl Becker, and Harry Elmer Barnes, might be discussed in the next lecture, "The Commitment to Scientific Explanation," for all these men believed that history could not be understood without reliance on the natural and social sciences. But what especially distinguished them—and this despite many differences among them—was their insistence that traditional historiography had overemphasized political and military events; it had failed to give due emphasis to the development of science, technology, and social science as well as to man's gift for cooperation in the public good. History as it could and should be written might clear the way for greater reliance on man's capacity to direct his future. Here the key was to be intellectual history, a largely, though not entirely, neglected theme.

As John Higham has pointed out, intellectual history requires an explicit view of the mind, and a view of the mind calls forth a view of human nature. If, to quote Higham, "the mind creates in ways that are neither bound by nor referable to the demands of an external environment—if ideas have a life of their own—then human nature bursts and transcends the patterns of the natural world around it. If, on the other hand, mind interests us as an agent of bio-social adaptation, we tend to assimilate human nature to an encompassing system of nature."[29] As I have suggested, the functional as opposed to the dualistic conception of mind was in the main the credo of the new historians.

Thus, these historians viewed human nature as neither rational nor irrational, but as sufficiently plastic to be capable of making new responses to new stimuli despite the pull of habit. This view implied a capacity for reshaping institutions and public life to improve individual and social behavior. Such a faith rested on a conception of how men think, learn, and relearn: in part by trial and error, in part by unconscious rationalizations of their interests and values, in part by creatively reaching for new solutions to impinging problems. The study of history could also play a role in men's thinking and behavior. As it had largely been written in the past, it tended to create the impression that exploitation, lust for power, war, or any existing institution, were the results of an innate quality in human nature.* Generally speaking,

---

*It is interesting to note the position that one of the leading "new" historians, Harry Elmer Barnes, took on the factors that brought about the two world wars. In his view, human agents did indeed figure in the responsibility for these events, but in response to

the new history maintained, to the contrary, that human nature does not reside in its products (custom, superstition, or the artificial products of human experience) but rather in the underlying strata of impulse and instinct out of which these finished products have developed. Despite the fact that human nature in this sense has encased itself in folkways and forms, it is to be thought of as essentially plastic. The trouble with historical scholarship was that it had given too little attention to the factors and forces that changed and directed these basic impulses, that is, science and scientific thinking, education, technology, and man's demonstrated capacity to cooperate for the public good. History as it could—and should—be written might clear the way for greater self-confidence in man's ability to direct his future. Such a written history would indeed remind men of the force of habit and of the possibility, on the basis of the historical record, of changing it. Thus, the new history assumed that war is an institutional crystallization of forces rather than a necessary expression of man's

---

personal shortcomings and to man-made institutions, such as nationalism and imperialism, not to human nature as such. On the other hand, Professor Dexter Perkins, a leading critic of the revisionist position in the scholarship of American diplomacy, held that "revisionism rests on a doubtful interpretation of human nature. Revisionists are often motivated by a dislike, perhaps even a noble dislike, of a resort to force. But, in fact, no institution is so deeply ingrained in human nature as war, and the attempt to flee from this fact is no solution to the age-old problem." *Foreign Policy and the American Spirit* (Ithaca, 1957), 94-105.

innate aggressiveness. It accepted from the new anthropology the idea that the apparent backwardness of certain races has resulted, not from innate differences, but from particular historical experiences.

It is possible here to discuss only one of the new historians, and I have chosen Charles A. Beard. He did not write biography, a genre in which the conception of human nature is most clearly evident. Nor did he write systematically about the idea of human nature. When he mentioned the term, it was within other contexts. Yet, it is not hard to reconstruct his view; unlike some of his historical positions, his view of human nature did not essentially change. If one were to try to account for Beard's conception of human nature, he would find shaping influences in his early environment, including his Quaker heritage, in the classics, particularly Aristotle and the Stoics, in Machiavelli, in Madison, Darwin, Lester Ward, and in the social scientists of the twentieth century, European and American.

Although Beard's thought about human nature was in harmony with aspects of social science that still seem to be valid, it transcended social science in its humanism and poetic vision. He expected less of human beings, whether in individual or group expression, than Robinson. His view left wide latitude for choice, individual and group, for Beard rejected the idea that human behavior in time can be reduced to a mathematical formula or understood by an analogy with physics or biology.

Yet Beard did not look on man as a completely free agent. He knew the conditioning role of geography, including natural resources. He also knew that heredity as well as environment limits man's activities. In the controversy over nature and nurture, he held that the two cannot be disentangled. Heredity and environment, he insisted, are inseparable phases of one organism, "criss-crossed and involuted through thousands of years of development." This of course is the language of functional psychology. Admitting that mental qualities are transmitted by inheritance, he held that these can be measured only in relation to environment—in the form of reactions to stimuli. "If we assume," he wrote, "that there is something transmitted down the centuries by inheritance without respect to environment, then where did the superior germ plasm come from? Was it specifically introduced by Almighty God in the beginning, or at some definite time later, and then carried uncontaminated down the sex stream? If so, how can we believe in evolution? On the other hand, if we believe in evolution, how can we escape the idea that environment and the struggle for existence have had a powerful influence on the conservable manifestations of the germ-plasm— of even the very best old primitive families?"[30]

Thus Beard rejected the doctrine that human nature inevitably points to an elite, whether based on sex, class, or race. He recognized, to be sure, the wide distribution of talents, including intelligence. But it is this wide distribution, with the great undistributed middle plateau, that strengthened his faith in democracy, however frail its historical expressions. This faith was further confirmed by his conviction that classes are not rooted in human nature, as his revered mentor James Madison supposed, but rather in historical circumstances. Thus, when it was fashionable in the 1920's to belittle the people for their alleged stupidity, Beard maintained that they have been sufficiently endowed to weather many a storm and to build the greatness of the Republic. Nor did he imagine that it is only the American people who possess enough native intelligence to govern themselves. He did not lay fascism at the door of human nature; he laid it, rather, at the door of historical developments.

Beard further emphasized the creative character of intelligent thinking—the capacity of men and women not only to think logically but to manipulate physical environment and to live decently and helpfully together. This they are enabled to do by virtue of such reinforcing native gifts as capacity for affection, loyalty, gratitude, and compassion. It is not clear whether Beard ascribed the moral sense, as Jefferson did, to man's original endowment, but he believed it to be deep, abiding, and crucial in the human make-up.

Yet, Beard never imagined human nature to be composed only of such desirable traits. He recognized opposing drives, including fear, avarice, pride, ambition, proclivity to violence, lust for power, and a seeming need for dependence on authority. He saw these drives as operating throughout history, and this insight informed many of his historical interpretations. Beard also took into account, on occasion, the unconscious, though only or largely as it operated in rationalization of personal or group interest. These frailties necessitated in the early phase of human history some kind of government, for, if men were angels, government would hardly have been needed. His admiration for *The Federalist* papers and for the Constitution, especially after the rise of totalitarianism, rested in part on his conviction that checks and balances are needed to prevent the more selfish components of human nature from getting the upper hand. Very early and throughout his years, he gave more than usual emphasis in his histories to social legislation, on the ground that men's intelligence, self-interest, and cooperative and kindly tendencies are insufficient in a modern technological society to overcome mass indifference and the proneness to submit to drift or even to manipulation.[31]

It is relevant to this discussion to consider only one of the many criticisms that have been made of Beard as a historian. Robert Skotheim has found an inconsistency in Beard's treatment of ideas and of how men developed and transmitted them. In Skotheim's view, Beard, in the 1930's, gave much greater consideration to the role of ideas in the historical process than he had earlier, whether because of his involvement in

the relativist controversy or because of his deeply
disturbed reaction to the challenge of totalitarianism to
humane and democratic values. Beard's inconsistency,
according to this critic, lay in his holding that con-
servative ideas are mere reflex rationalizations of the
interests of the *status quo* and, on the other hand, in
his giving a largely autonomous role to the origin of
ideas associated with the challenge that science,
democracy, progress, and civilization presented.[32]

These criticisms misread, I think, Beard's understanding of the nature and function of ideas in relation
to human nature. Throughout his whole career he
thought in terms of the functional psychology and the
instrumentalist philosophy. "It is evident," he wrote,
"all about us and in the records of history that idea and
interest, thought and deed, evolve together."[33] The
creative thinker is not completely emancipated from
all conditioning circumstances; he is unable to make
new ideas and new chapters in history merely out of
his imagination and without reference to concrete
realities. Ideas, whether traditional and functional to
the rationalization of an established order or challenging and creative, are to be regarded as plans of
action for problem-solving that develop, not separately
and as mental images, but as part of the responses of
the adjusting human organism. Actually, Beard never
—even in his later period—assumed that ideas develop and are transmitted apart from human agents
responding in one or another way to problems in

their environment. He saw, not a monolithic environment in which ideas are either mere reflex rationalizations of interests or entirely autonomous mental images; rather, he conceived of society as complex if not pluralistic, as dynamic, not static. In meeting social problems that challenge established institutions, critics, social reformers, and social scientists project proposed new solutions in the form of ideas that differ from the given, inherited ones that at an earlier time and in a different context had themselves been responses to emerging changes. At the same time, the criticism of Beard for making traditional ideas dependent reflexes and for giving autonomy to new and challenging ones that seemed to function independently of actualities obscures his consistent conception of "interests" as embracing economic *and* psychological factors. Probably much of the controversy about Beard's work would not have arisen had he clearly and explicitly offered an adequate psychological theory that explicitly made economic and acquisitive values instrumentally functional to definite uses and ends within a naturalistic frame.[34]

It is ironical that Beard, with these views of human nature, evident in his historical writing and important to his historical interpretations, has in some quarters been regarded as a dangerous, debunking, and materialistic cynic. The truth is that he strongly believed in the power of values, ideals, and intelligence to guide man to a realization of at least some of his better potentialities. At the same time, he did not find in the record any overwhelming evidence pointing to easy optimism, for Beard was deeply impressed by the role in history of accident, contingency, or fate, or by the interplay of variables. If the gate to improving the common lot could be kept open, there was nothing in the past, Beard thought, that provided reassuring proof that man could not find his way through.

The idea that man's fate is not determined by the limitations of human nature has more recently influenced the writing of a group of younger historians who may be called "revisionists." I can cite here only two or three examples. In the 1920's and 1930's specialists on the Civil War argued that this great catastrophe resulted from the blundering of the leaders and from the failure of the great majority, endowed with compassion and peaceful desires, to check the fanatically emotional extremists in both North and South. After the impact of totalitarianism, especially Nazism, on public thought, such historians among a still younger generation of historians as Arthur M. Schlesinger, Jr., revised the revisionists by insisting that crises emerge in which great moral issues are at stake and that man's inborn or at least deeply embedded moral impulses must be invoked on the side of righteousness even if this leads, as it did in 1861, to war. That this position was in part a reaction to and justification of the American challenge to totalitarianism in the Second World War and, perhaps, to the Cold War, is a legitimate inference.

One ought also to note that in the writing of the history of the African American a great change has taken place in the last two decades, coincident with the civil rights movement and the racial revolution. Emphasis has recently been placed on the essential similarities in the make-up of blacks and whites. One well-known authority has argued that the Negroes are, in effect, white men with black skins.[35] Others have emphasized the influence of slavery in inhibiting the Negro's capacity for developing his talents and have explained Uncle Tomism as a function of slavery comparable to the cowed and ingratiating behavior of some victims of Nazi concentration camps.[36] On the other hand, emphasis has also been put by such historians as Aptheker, Franklin, Meier, and Butcher on the militancy of Negroes throughout their American experience and on their extraordinary achievements even in slavery and in the atmosphere of discrimination that has marked the years from emancipation to our own time.[37] All these tendencies in recent historical interpretation reflect not only a relationship between historians and changing situations but also a still living faith in the capacity of human nature to play a significant role in shaping the American present and future.

III
THE COMMITMENT TO SCIENTIFIC EXPLANATION

THE MOVEMENT for the scientific writing of history in nineteenth-century Germany and its transit to America are too well known to warrant more than the barest summary. Negatively, it was a reaction against the heritage of history as a branch of literature. It was also a reaction against the propensity of many eighteenth-century writers to conceive of history as teaching by example, that is, of history as a normative and even propagandistic exercise in morality. On the positive side, the new movement was influenced by the Cartesian revolution and by the great achievements of natural science in the modern era. The exponents of scientific history assumed, like the natural scientists, that objectivity is the hallmark of science. In the minds of the leading exponents of scientific history, their purpose could be achieved by the skillful and careful use of prescribed methods in the assessment of documents and records and by the detachment of practitioners from the influences of the time and place in which they wrote. At least in the first stage of the new movement, some exponents also assumed that, through the proper study of the past, general historical laws might be discovered, as verifiable and as certain as those of the natural sciences. The search for general laws tended to de-emphasize an explicit idea about human nature that, despite Darwin, was generally assumed to be a constant. An image of man nevertheless, at least by implication, crept into their work. Of late some historians, in quest of an enlargement of the scientific component of their craft, have self-consciously turned to the behavioral sciences. In addition to their emphasis on method these have sometimes worked within a conceptual frame related to one or another theory of human nature.

It would be possible to discuss the first really great American exponent of the scientific movement in historical thought and writing within the terms of my first lecture—the limitations of man's capacities—for, however muted, Henry Adams' image of man reflected his monistic, materialistic, mechanistic, and pessimistic world view, the idea, in brief, that man is merely a pawn in the cosmic chess game. But it is more meaningful, I believe, to take Henry Adams at his own estimate—as a historian who hewed to the scientific method in historical writing. The problem then becomes, in the main, that of exploring the extent to which such views of human nature as he expressed or as are implied in his historical scholarship issued inexorably from the evidence he presented or derived rather from his temperament, his relation to his age as he conceived that relationship, and his world view.[1]

One of Henry Adams' contemporaries, Oliver Wendell Holmes, Jr., always insisted that the lawyer arrived at general principles only through disciplined application of his mind to particular instances; a lawyer had to become a specialist, Holmes maintained, perhaps with all the more vehemence because his age was one in which, in some ways at least, the tendency to generalize was in vogue. Henry Adams had very much the same attitude toward historical scholarship that Holmes had toward the law. The study of history required what Adams called the "philosophic method," a synonym, as he used the term, for the scientific method. In a letter to his friend Charles Milnes Gaskell, Adams wrote of the scholar employing this method that he "delights in studying phenomena, whether of his own mind or matter, with absolute indifference to the results. His business is to reason about life, thought, the soul, and truth, as though he were reasoning about phosphates and square roots; and to a mind fairly weary of self, there is a marvelous relief and positive delight in getting down to the hard pan of science. He never stops to ask what the result of a theory or demonstration is to be on his own relations to God or to life. His pleasure is to work as though he were a small God and immortal and possibly omniscient."[2] Adams' emphasis on "getting down to the hard pan of science," or on concentrating one's attention on the particular problem involved rather than worrying about the consequences of any result for one's "relations to God or to life," represents basically the same sort of distinction that Holmes made between specialization and generalization. The investigator must concentrate on the task at hand, stoically, and take toll later on.

In Adams' case, as in Holmes's, this attitude constituted more than a mere methodology. It pervaded his whole outlook on life, resulting in what might be called tough-mindedness. Thus, Adams wrote to Henry Cabot Lodge, a member of his famous Harvard seminar in the 1870's, that "there is only one way to look at life, and that is the practical way. Keep clear of mere sentiment whenever you have to decide a practical question. Sentiment is very attractive and I like it as well as most people, but nothing in the way of action is worth much if it is not practically sound. The question is whether the historico-literary line is practically worth following, not whether it will amuse or improve you. Can you make it *pay*?"[3]

As we might expect, the historical method appropriate to this tough-minded, stoical attitude toward the profession itself required an extraordinary degree of "objectivity" on the part of the historian. In a later letter to Lodge, Adams emphasized the importance of mastering the scientific method and of adopting "the rigid principle of subordinating everything to perfect thoroughness of study." In this the example of the German historical school was especially commended. Adams' preoccupation with objectivity or "practicality," a term that was, as he used it, virtually synonymous with objectivity, extended even to the choice of subject. "The mere wish to give a practical turn to my men [students] has almost necessarily led me to give a strong legal bent to the study." After elaborating some of his own findings concerning medieval legal institutions, Adams observed that there was really no historical subject that could be isolated from the others; the history of law or of philology, of America or Europe or even Egypt fascinated Adams equally because it was less the subject than the method that drew him to history and that he mainly wanted to teach his students. "It matters very little what line you take provided you can catch the tail of an idea to develop with solid reasoning and thorough knowledge. America or Europe, our own century or prehistoric time, are all alike to the historian if he can only find out what men are and have been driving at, consciously or unconsciously."[4]

This discussion of Adams' conception of methodology

may seem somewhat removed from the role of human nature in his historical thinking, but on the whole it is pertinent. It gives us an idea of what he was consciously attempting in his historical research. His method, in brief, demanded the highest possible degree of objectivity. It led him to select subjects on the basis of their lack of contemporary appeal and even to deny the importance of subject to the historian's task. If this is a fair representation of Adams' purpose, it should be possible to find the roles an idea of human nature *might* have played in his history.

It should be quite clear, first of all, that a historian trying to do what Adams attempted would not be inclined to exploit "the moral potential" of history with respect to human nature. David Ramsay and Mercy Warren had found, and James Harvey Robinson and his associates in the New History were to find great moral significance in recent history and the need to dramatize that significance for the moral improvement of their audience and of society. For Adams, of course, moral sentiments had no place in historical writing. Furthermore, recent history, precisely because of its apparent relevance, provides the wrong sort of subject altogether. The historian is a scientist, not a propagandist, however clearly he might see no incompatibility between the two roles.

The second alternative, the use of a scientific view of human nature—or what passed for one—as a tool of objective analysis of the past, might at first seem to

Adams a more likely choice. In 1871, when he began his teaching at Harvard, he was familiar with the older psychologically oriented writers, including Descartes, Pascal, and the eighteenth-century monistic materialists, Cabanis, Condillac, and Helvétius. Of his contemporaries among the psychologically bent writers he knew Taine, whose *Théorie de l'Intelligence* he chose for notice in the *North American Review*, which he was editing. Realizing that contemporary psychology was "a new study, and a dark corner in education," he acquainted himself with such leading British exponents of physiological psychology as Maudsley and Bain, and, though he did not read James's *Principles* until after his own first historical writing had been finished, it is safe to assume that he was familiar with the functionalist psychology William James was teaching and communicating in many articles before *The Principles* (1890) appeared.[5] Nor is this all, for Adams often insisted that man had to be analyzed scientifically. Indeed, he was outspoken in his antagonism to a society that was "ready to brand as doctrinaire everyone who talks about applying [science] to the affairs of men." In his book notices in the *North American Review* Adams warmly praised those authors with the "courage to come before the world" with the findings of such scientific analysis.[6]

We can understand why this enthusiasm failed to result in an explicit, organized view of human nature in Adams' historical work only if we recognize that for him the application of science to human affairs meant primarily the study of sociological arrangements and the validation of sociological laws—as with Auguste Comte, an influence on his thought in this early period. Adams' assumption that sociological laws derive from and are consonant with the laws of the universe as nineteenth-century physicists envisioned them reflected his move from biology to physics. Thus, human nature itself, in the psychological sense in which it was understood by the Wundtian and other biologically oriented psychologists of the day, was for Adams merely a function of cosmic forces. His thinking developed after science had taken a firm hold on American intellectual life but before the new psychology had become prestigious. His famous dialogue with William James on free will, carried on by correspondence in 1882, indicated the way in which his thought was tending.[7] In arguing for unqualified determinism Adams was denying the basic premise on which psychology is based: that the human mind has at least a limited amount of intrinsic importance in the affairs of men. The result in Adams' written history was a tendency to treat all human events, including personalities, as mere functions of sociological and, ultimately, physical laws.

If Henry Adams was more intrigued by the search for universal laws than by an effort to fathom human nature in and for itself or as a key to history, it would be wrong to conclude that he did not make use of a concept of human nature both in his biographies and in *The History of the United States*. Like others in his day, he used the term *human nature* without adequately defining it, but we can surmise his understanding. His reference to instincts as innate in human nature and his statement that man's capacity for reason and logic had not increased materially over the ages implied a static or unchanging concept of human nature. Indeed, after exploring the theory of evolution he concluded that it did not bear out the notion of organic progress and that, in any case, the acceleration of the tempo of change in the American experience made it irrelevant to any discussion of the American man.

More helpful is Adams' explicit rejection of one view of human nature. In 1875, in a review of a new edition of George Bancroft's *History of the United States,* Adams spoke deprecatingly of the author's "genteel feelings of humanity" and noted that the rise of Jacksonian Democracy, which had so greatly influenced Bancroft, actually revealed the "immeasurable depths of human selfishness."[8] In his own *History* Adams ascribed many of the failures of President Jefferson—and to a lesser extent those of Gallatin—to an inadequate appreciation of "the force and complexity of the human passions and instincts."[9] In acting on the naive and unrealistic view that man is endowed with an ability, through reason, to see his own and the national self-interest and in ignoring the force of vanity and habit in the human condition, Jefferson invited his troubles. The error became notably evident when his well-intentioned but unrealistic statesmanship downgraded the importance of force as an instrument of national policy when that policy was challenged by the greater power and realism of Old World antagonists. Jefferson's heroic failure, for all its dignity and tragedy, was a failure common to those holding a similarly inadequate image of man.[10] (This might be Reinhold Niebuhr speaking.)

On the positive side, Adams explicitly spoke of the higher and lower aspects of human nature and held that successful public policy must take both into account. Among the higher aspects Adams included man's capacity for rationality and an emotional endowment that expresses itself in the capacity for self-sacrifice, heroism, compassion, religion, and creative imagination; among the lower aspects he included aggressiveness, selfishness, lust for power, self-deception, vanity, and proneness to corruption. All these traits are mixed together in any member of the human kind, in varying proportions. Let me give a few instances of Adams' use of human nature as an instrument of historical interpretation.

Examples of behavior that was contrary to self-interest, however apparent to reason and common sense, included the Federalists' opposition to the Embargo from which they profited, the complacency of

Virginians toward it even when it was obviously ruining them, the failure of the restless New Orleans creoles to make a real rebellion against the United States, and the endurance of General Harrison's mistreated, hungry, and trapped soldiers.[11] The War of 1812 both "opened the sluices of human corruption" and, with all its horrors, proved that "war could purify as well as debase; it . . . taught courage, discipline and the stern sense of duty," which are also potentialities of human nature.[12] And, elsewhere, the revealing statement of the elitist Adams stands: "Democracies in history always suffered from the necessity of uniting with much of the purest and best in human nature a mass of ignorance and brutality lying at the bottom of all societies."[13]

Associated with all these kinds of conduct was, of course, motivation. In Adams' own words, "motives were enigmas too obscure for search."[14] Yet, he came close to ascribing motives in his treatment of some of the leading figures in his historical writing. When he did, it is open to question whether what he said stemmed inexorably from the documents, or from his view of human nature, or from the interaction of the two. Overarching all the comments and implications, however, was the fairly consistent commitment to psychological determinism. The only freedom of will men really had was the freedom to agree with forces more powerful than men, or to be wrecked by them.[15]

Whatever actual and potential qualities Adams

thought all peoples or races share in common, he believed, like most late nineteenth-century historians, that racial differences are sufficiently marked to explain varying institutions and national character itself. In the case of America he concluded that the development of its national character was inevitable and, as he wrote in 1876 in a joint review of von Holst's *History of the United States,* an evidence of the "symmetry and real majesty of force" operating in the mode of the mechanical action of nature herself.[16] But national character could change, as the developments between 1800 and 1817 suggested. These developments had to do with the accelerated use of energy, whether in military potentiality, or in the application of technology to the exploitation of resources, or in the expanding drive of individual citizens. In the American experience Adams saw reason, on the one hand, for concluding that a democratic republic could not avoid the age-old brutalities and tragedies of mankind and, on the other, special circumstances associated in part with the peculiarities of American democracy that, in relation to Europe, subordinated personalities to mass. Thus, in America he saw an opportunity to understand the evolution of a race that the historian of Europe could not match. America, in offering a more restricted field for the development of individuality than older and smaller societies, testified to an achievement of a higher *average* of intelligence, or acuteness, or smartness.

Moreover, "even the wicked became less mischievous in an atmosphere where virtue was easier than vice. Punishments seemed mild in a society where every offender could cast off his past, and create a new career."[17] Yet, there seemed no real warrant for believing that the American actually achieves a higher morality than exists elsewhere. If there is nothing in the record to warrant belief in an "endlessly upward" march of progress, Adams nevertheless concluded that, "stripped for the hardest work, every muscle firm and elastic, every ounce of brain ready for use, not a trace of superfluous flesh on his nervous and supple body, the American stood in the world a new order of man."[18] Yet, there is little that is heroic in the American man: the hero counts for little; the individual is important chiefly as a representative type.

But these and other generalizations are rare, inasmuch as Adams on the whole did adhere to his creed that the facts must speak for themselves. In addition to such evidences as I have cited of explicit generalization, one can profitably pay close attention to the tone of certain crucial passages, to the tenses chosen, and to the images used to summarize developments. An example is the concluding paragraph of Adams' chapter on "The Intellect of New England" in 1800. After describing New England's aristocratic-Calvinistic culture when confronted by the steady progress of democratic principles in the Southern and Middle states, Adams went on to say, "Evidently an intellectual con-

dition like that of New England could not long continue. The thoughts and methods of the eighteenth
century held possession of men's minds only because
the movement of society was delayed by political
passions. Massachusetts, and especially Boston, already
contained a younger generation eager to strike into
new paths, while forcibly held in the old ones. The
more decidedly the college graduates of 1800 disliked
democracy and its habits of thought, the more certain
they were to compensate for political narrowness by
freedom in fields not political. The future direction of
the New England intellect seemed already suggested
by the impossibility of going further in the line of
President Dwight and Fisher Ames. Met by a barren
negation on that side, thought was driven to some new
channel; and the United States were the more concerned in the result because, with the training and
literary habits of New Englanders and the new models
already established in Europe for their guidance, they
were likely again to produce something that would
command respect."[19] First let us consider the over-all
tone of the passage, Adams' use of the past tense
and the passive voice: According to one theory of
history the job of the practitioner is to bring the
past to new life in the present; Adams seems, by contrast, almost to perform an autopsy on the past, to
be less the historian, more the histologist. Second,
consider the way men's feelings, in this case the
"political passions" of New England Federalism, can

delay the "movement of society" but really cannot positively affect it. In this respect Adams reminds one of William Graham Sumner, who always insisted that men could make society worse but could never make it better. Third, and most significant, perhaps, consider the way in which in this passage Adams subtly communicates his conviction that thought is determined and, in substance, no different from any other material. Faced with a "barren" environment, *intellect* cannot survive. Like water, *thought* is "driven to some new channel." And like any other sort of material, New England *culture* is molded by a combination of "habit" in association with "new models."

Adams professed great dissatisfaction with his overall achievement in *The History*—it demonstrated, he wrote, the inadequacies of the scientific emphasis on the detached procedure of letting the facts speak for themselves.[20] Most of his later historical writing sought for laws. The most impressive ones he arrived at were his generalization as to the success of the twelfth century in achieving a sense of unity in the balance of reason and feeling and his concept of the dissipation of energy and the rule of phase. Apart from *Mont-Saint-Michel and Chartres* (1904), the conception of human nature is so obscured and even negated (for a rare exception, see *The Education*, 474) by his emphasis on the relation of force, mass, and acceleration to stages of development in man's story that we need not, in the context of our theme, linger over these much-written-about theories and laws.[21] It is relevant, however, to note that in his first and most impressive efforts Adams hardly succeeded in basing his generalizations, at least as to human nature, on his own scientific ideal and on methods he shared with the von Ranke school of objective history. What he did, rather, was to reflect his own disenchantment with the Gilded Age as he saw his place in it. His views of human nature derived from this self-image of his role, from his temperament, from the ideas about human nature drawn from his heritage, and from his reactions to currents of philosophical and psychological thought in his maturing years.

It was only rarely that a later historian in the scientific school tried to derive general laws, and these efforts were hardly successful. Yet the endeavor of an important group of historians to carry the scientific approach further than that represented by the von Ranke school must be noted and in some part evaluated.

Of the movements of thought of the nineteenth and early twentieth centuries those associated with Marx and Freud promised, at least in the minds of their exponents, new and important scientific tools. Each differed from and in many ways was antagonistic to the other. But both opened doors, hitherto only slightly ajar, and thereby revealed misunderstandings of available historical record and provided correctives to the effects of the historian's own personal equation.

Marx emphasized the deep and pervading—because unconscious—rationalizations of class values that distorted what he thought to be objective reality. Freud, with other tools and insights, provided a new sense and awareness of the unconscious motives of human actions regardless of class: to name only the more important, the sex drive; conflicts in early life over the authority of the father and the ego of the child, often repressed and leading to feelings of inferiority or inadequacy; desire for power and authority; ineptness in the use of these if and when acquired; and compensatory behavior; or, put differently, the idea that man is not only largely nonrational but also, because of the ambiguous and contradictory relationships to the civilization he created, a neurotic animal as well. These new movements of thought were seldom accepted outright in the historical profession as keys to interpretation, but both exerted an indirect influence of considerable importance: It was no longer possible for the historian to assume that he stood, neutral and objective, outside of himself and his society, as he investigated historical record. I must here confine my comments mainly to those historians who explicitly accepted one or both of these ideologies or, if one prefers, tools, under the assumption that they were important if not indispensable as well as neglected scientific handmaids.

Inasmuch as the Marxist conceptualizations subordinated personality and individual behavior to historical materialism and a dialectical class struggle, it would be hard to test, so far as the idea of human nature in history goes, the claim that Marxism is the only validly scientific tool. Nor would one even expect to find an emphasis on or even perhaps a recognition of the idea of human nature as such in Marxist historical scholarship. There are indeed important insights into the role of fear in antebellum interracial tensions and into the kinds of personalities the capitalist system presumably required. But I do not find in the historical writings of A. M. Simons, Lewis Corey, Philip Foner, Herbert Aptheker, and other American Marxist historians much that is really relevant to our subject. It is, moreover, an open question whether the Marxist impact has promoted the objective freedom from the influence of class rationalizations that the canon promised. But it does stand as a caveat against the unconscious rationalizing influences of the bourgeois cultural heritage and of the middle-class historian's place in our society.

A more complex issue involves the usefulness of psychoanalysis for a deeper if not a unique understanding of the psychic factors in historical processes as these bear on the conception of human nature. Despite the provocative suggestions of Harry Elmer Barnes in the 1920's and the noteworthy address that William Langer, a distinguished diplomatic historian, presented as president of the American Historical Association in 1957,[22] the chief efforts to use psychoanalysis for probing the larger and more complex kinds of collective behavior have been those of nonprofessional scholars. No one should discount Lewis Mumford's impressive historical synthesis of the development of the city, bogged down as it has been with explosive anxieties, creative as it has been in its cultural contributions. A few historians have been favorably impressed by the efforts of Herbert Marcuse, Bruce Mazlish, and Norman O. Brown, who have given us somewhat pretentious expositions of culture over time, with commentaries on the nature of man. John Burnham, a professional historian well grounded in psychoanalysis, concluded that such analyses of the psychic aspects of historical process and of collective behavior have hardly proved very useful.[23]

To this informed judgment there are exceptions. Dixon Wecter, in his study *The Hero in America*, concluded that the crowds unconsciously wish for heroes with whom they can identify, heroes whose salty, sacrificial taste of disappointment and even of tragedy corresponds with the life they have known.[24] To cite another example, David B. Davis has made effective use of the psychoanalytical concepts of sex, fear, insecurity, transfer, and projection in an analysis of what he calls the countersubversive themes of the anti-Masonic, anti-Catholic, and anti-Mormon behaviors in the second third of the nineteenth century. These widely held fears and denunciations cannot be entirely explained in terms of stimulus-response prejudices, ethnic tensions, and status rivalries; also involved were irrational myths and stereotypes of a common enemy who was plotting subversion against American democratic values and conspiring against the millennial visions of American glory as well as against the sacred heritage of the past. In a period of bewildering change the countersubversive behavior of great numbers of Americans reflected both a fear and an envy of the enemy's alleged sexual expressions, repressed in their own lives, preoccupation with themes of guilt and confession, and near-paranoia. If the documentation does not meet every historian's criteria, Davis found sufficient explicit evidence in the literary record to reduce inference to plausible dimensions.[25]

Two other examples of the use of psychoanalytical theory to explain collective behavior may be mentioned. One has been an interest in the psychology of slavery. The much-discussed thesis of Stanley Elkins has argued that the institution induced a docility comparable to that resulting from the imprisonment of Jews in Nazi concentration camps.[26] Recently, Earl E. Thorpe has challenged this view by holding that the personalities of slaves varied greatly and by contending that slavery can best be understood in its psychological aspects by keeping in mind the frequent incidence of affection on the side of both blacks and owners in a familial relationship and the nonrepressive effects of the institution on the sex impulses of everyone except white women, an exception related to fears identified as the castration complex.[27] Both positions rest largely on historical analogy, common-sense insight, and undocumented application of psychoanalytic theory. The second main example of the use of this theory for explaining collective behavior is the analysis of the Populist and Progressive movements in terms of anxiety-status conflict, but this can better be discussed in relation to new uses of social science concepts in efforts to explain collective behavior.

Historians have used psychoanalytic concepts much more frequently in biographical writing. In the second decade of our own century, when Freud, Jung, and their disciples were just beginning to be known in America, Preserved Smith and Ralph V. Harlow, historians ill-equipped for the task, adopted Freudian and Adlerian concepts, only to abandon the experiment in their later work, perhaps because their initial efforts met with indifference or harsh criticism. More recently, however, a number of historians, better equipped and often more modest in their claims, have undertaken the task, with results that can be tentatively assessed in terms of their contributions and limitations as a scientific handmaid for an understanding of human nature. I use the term *scientific* with reservations, for I am aware that most academic psychologists have questioned the scientific validity of generalizations and applications based on theory alone or, at best, on clinical evidence.

In these later studies, as in those of the pioneers, the dominant focus has been on the problem of motivation. Almost all of the subjects chosen have been historically important because of their radical protests against the Establishment. Preserved Smith, whose scholarly and conventional *Life and Letters of Martin Luther* (1911) explained the Protestant leader's revolt in terms of "a torturing sense of sin and a longing for reconciliation with God," advanced, in an article published in 1913, the thesis that Luther's frustrations and unhappiness as a child and youth, the results of his hatred of an authoritative and domineering father, led to inner struggles, an obsession with sex, and self-inflicted asceticism that in the end were channeled into defiance of the authority of the Church.[28] More recently the distinguished psychiatrist Erik Erikson, using much the same material, has qualified and refined this analysis by emphasizing the importance of Luther's identity crisis and its functional relationship to a larger, concrete, and changing historical situation.[29] The second historical pioneer was Ralph V. Harlow. His life of Samuel Adams explained the rebel's radicalism as a defensive and compensatory reaction to his perception of his father's tangles with British authorities and to his own early failures in business enterprise.[30]

The same kind of childhood conflicts with parental authority and alienation from the family, thoroughly repressed and channeled into subsequent behavior patterns, has informed other biographies. Woodrow Wilson's repressed sense of inadequacy and inferiority toward his well-meaning but domineering clerical father has been seen as the key to his subsequent compensatory desire to affirm his self-esteem and to vindicate himself in a quest for power and leadership in crusades challenging domestic and international patterns of authority.[31] In a somewhat similar vein Thaddeus Stevens' radical abolitionism has been seen as an expression of his "inner desperate needs" that, in turn, sprang unconsciously from his wish to compensate for the effects on his life of a drunken, irresponsible father and for his own clubfoot handicap.[32] Likewise, Charles Sumner's antislavery radicalism has been explained as a partial result of an ego drive, neurotic compulsions, and a martyr complex as well as of a capacity for self-deception, all of which, allegedly, were rooted in his early life experiences.[33] These interpretations have been challenged on the score of an excessive reliance on theory in lieu of documentation impossible to secure. They have also been challenged on the ground that such attributions assume that protest against human evil can be made only by neurotic behavior, that such neuroticism was not true of many abolitionists, and, further, that there is increasing evidence, both in psychoanalysis and in experimental psychology, that the motivation for many protest decisions is grounded in intelligent and rational commitment, especially in a democratic culture, when obvious human suffering is clearly a result of a social institution.

Other examples of the recent use by historians of psychoanalytical theories may be mentioned, one of which, Emery Battis' *Saints and Sectaries* (1962), also makes use of sociological analysis. Here the crucial key to Mrs. Anne Hutchinson's religious radicalism is found in her unsatisfied search for masculine authority, initially evident in her relations with her father and in the end in her direct relations with God, together with the immediately precipitating anxieties of menopause. The accompanying analysis of the motivations of her disciples rules out manifest economic advantage and offers no psychological explanation.[34]

Two other examples fall within the period of the American Revolution. Professor Richard L. Bushman, in an original and acute analysis of Benjamin Franklin's *Autobiography*, has shown that key passages provide evidence of a relationship between his subject's involvements with father and elder brother and his developing behavior pattern. Franklin met the problem of hostility deftly and self-consciously by seeking to avoid or bypass conflict or, when that failed, to manage a working reconciliation by shifting the elements of the conflicting situation.[35] The other study, which I find to be the most impressive of all, is the collaborative effort of Dr. Frederick Wyatt and William B. Willcox, a psychiatrist and a historian thoroughly in control of the documentary and manuscript materials, to explain a personality conflict that contributed to the British failure to subdue the American Revolutionists.[36] The mass of evidence for the American career of Sir Henry Clinton, commander of the British forces, evidence singularly rich in contrast with the complete lack of information for his background and early life, seemed to Professor Willcox inadequate to explain, on any rational or manifest grounds, Sir Henry's constant quarrels with associates, his failure, when a subordinate, to persuade his superiors to accept his proposals, and his similar failure, when he had the supreme command he so eagerly had sought, to carry through his plans. It seemed plausible to hypothesize that this ambiguous dichotomy in Clinton's personality stemmed from an unconscious conflict with authority in his early life. With much caution the collaborating scholars tested this hypothesis with all the evidence at hand for Sir Henry's mature years. They concluded, modestly and tentatively, that the hypothesis was sustained by the evidence, without any imposition of the pre-projected hypothesis.[37] The strength of the analysis derives in large part from Professor Willcox's mastery of his historical material and from the critical awareness of pitfalls on the part of the associated psychiatrist. The analysis explains much that escaped such earlier historians as Bancroft, Channing, Miller, and Ward. In providing a plausible explanation of motivation when traditional historical methods offered no light, this study suggests that, for certain problems, psychoanalytical tools and concepts, carefully and competently used, can extend and deepen the historian's understanding of human nature both as an idea and as a substantive reality in influencing past events.

It remains to consider the effect of the behavioral sciences on historical scholarship insofar as this impact bears on the idea of human nature. One must straight off make clear that the very concept of human nature seems irrelevant to the behavioral scientists and to historians who have been influenced by them. Human nature as an idea seems, like historical forces and other abstractions employed for historical explanation, much too vague, general, and lacking in precise definition as well as too complex to be a useful concept. Nevertheless, the thinking and work of the historians who have been in some way influenced by the behavioral sciences have, whether they are aware of it or not, added a new dimension to the theme with which we are concerned.

Historians who have worked with the concepts and procedures of the behavioral scientists have shared with them a dissatisfaction with the limits imposed on the search for scientific objectivity by the idea of relativism. On the positive side these scholars have been much influenced by logical positivism. Its canons of course include insistence on precise definitions and on neutral terms in analytical procedures in order to counteract "the tyranny of persuasive rhetoric." Also emphasized is the critical analysis of concepts or ways of looking at a subject. This analysis involves precise concern with the combinations of phenomena designated by a particular concept. Assumptions are examined in somewhat the same way and larger questions are broken down into manageable units in the interest of satisfactory explanation and validation. In addition to these canons, a few historians have extended the boundaries of analysis by the use of explanatory models. These include, in addition to quantification of data for controlling variables, the use of carefully defined historical analogies when intermediate variables are nonquantifiable, the extension of the rules of evidence from individual to mass behavior, and reliance on career profiles, role playing, and reference groups. Let me briefly indicate a few examples of how these ideas and procedures illuminate motivation and behavior.

One of the first intensive historical inquiries within this frame was the work that my associates and I did on a Wisconsin county, published under the title *The Making of an American Community* (1959). It was possible to define precisely the cultural groups in terms of nativity, religious affiliation, educational achievements, occupations, and economic status, not only in a given year, but over several decades. By computer control we were able to determine the relative importance of place of birth, age, sex, education, and economic status in marriage patterns, in promoting and sustaining leaders, in voting behavior, and in the decisions to stay in the county or to try again in more promising areas farther west. By controlling variables it was possible, then, to establish with mathematical precision the probable behavior of members of defined cultural groups.

Similar questions as well as more far-ranging ones have been explored with a good deal of success by Lee Benson, Stephan Thernstrom, and Thomas C. Cochran, to name only three. Thanks to Benson we can now conclude that, at least in New York State, Jacksonian Democracy is a misleading concept, in that Jackson men often opposed egalitarian and humanitarian programs and that the voting behavior of the less advantaged groups was determined less by economic status than by ethnic, religious, and other factors.[38] Thanks to Thernstrom we now know that in at least one nineteenth-century Massachusetts community, Newburyport, there is no solid basis in fact for the widely held view that social mobility was a significant reality.[39] We now know that we have no credible evidence for assessing the influence of what is loosely and almost meaninglessly called public opinion on the decisions that led to the Civil War.[40] On the positive side, Professor Cochran has shown the importance in decision-making of role playing and of reference groups among key railroad executives in the nineteenth century. Professor Cochran has also established probable relationships in the shifts from entrepreneurship to managerial patterns and to mass production by the skillful use of a model involving role expectations, cultural conditioning of model personality types, reference groups, and carefully defined historical analogies with business behavior in Latin-American culture.[41]

The usefulness of what I have called the behavioral science approach to historical explanation is nicely illustrated in the criticism Robert Doherty has made of the status-anxiety concept. This, it may be recalled, was used by Hofstadter, Donald, and other historians to explain radical protest behavior. The revolution in the distribution of power and prestige through rapid social and economic change, the thesis goes, explains why those whose status was lowered or threatened became reformers. For the most part, those using this explanation failed adequately to break down into testable units the broad and general concepts of environment and status and to use control groups and comparative techniques. The thesis, in short, assumed the validity of the intervening variables or, in different words, that shifts in power and prestige stemmed from the environment and that anxiety stemmed from status. Doherty proposed, in addition to defining groups in specific environments and to using control groups, a model in which the concepts of social role and reference groups might be used to test the intervening variables. He did not claim to have solved the problem, but he did, I think, show more clearly than others why the thesis is inadequate and how different techniques might fruitfully inform further empirical investigation.[42]

All this may actually, of course, be less innovative than it appears to be. It seems clear, however, that these approaches to historical explanation offer a scientific handmaid that introduces a new chapter in the history of historical thought about human nature. The concept can no longer be used, as many historians did use it, without adequate definition or as a convenient abstraction. An awareness and understanding of the factors entering into perception of self and of others and into the motivation of actions has already advanced historical inquiry and explanation into more scientific and objective channels. What has been done may well be only a beginning.

This exploration of the idea of human nature in American historical thought has rested on a selection of historians over the past three centuries. The historians chosen seem to be representative in many ways of the main emphases in the conceptions of history in their time, though, to be sure, each historian reflects in some ways the influence of his own background, experience, personality, and scholarship. Each of the historians about whom I have spoken has, in his writing, reflected a view of the nature of man, in some cases explicitly, in a larger number of instances indirectly and implicitly. Broadly speaking, these views corresponded to one or to another of the images

of man accessible in the cultural heritage and the prevailing or competing views of human nature at a given
time. To be sure, my analysis shows that the views of
human nature of these historians represent a combination of ideas rather than a simple borrowing from
any single, easily labeled school of thought. At the
same time, some of the changing emphases reflect
responses to such movements of thought as Puritanism,
the Enlightenment, the romantic impulse and Transcendentalism, nineteenth-century science, and, later,
the new functional psychology and psychoanalysis.
Yet, with the exception of Niebuhr, none of these historians seem, in their work, to have been consistently
informed by any systematic or specialized analysis of
human nature. Most historians used the term in a common-sense way. The uses that these historians made
of the general and abstract conceptions of human nature broaden and deepen our understanding of shifts
in the reputation of human nature over time and thus
expand our knowledge of a little-explored but important concept in the history of Western thought. But
perhaps the larger significance of our inquiry lies in
the trend we have discovered away from the common-
sense view of human nature toward a view developed
from the use of science.

Most of the historians, I suspect, supposed that such
views of human nature as they expressed or implied
stemmed from the evidence. Few, it seems, were aware
of the role of their own experience and assumptions

in the interpretation of evidence, in attributing motives, or in constructing syntheses. Nevertheless, judgments of the motivation and behavior of historical figures and the larger generalizations, especially about national character, rested in part on these personal views and assumptions interacting with social contexts.

The term *human nature* still appears in philosophical, theological, and literary discussion, but we seldom meet with it now in historical writing. In recent decades historians in general have simply avoided the use of abstract assumptions about the nature of man and have begun to use new tools and concepts to deepen and sharpen our understanding of man's behavior and, through his behavior, of his nature. The findings so far seem amoral, at least in contrast with the implications of human nature as formerly understood. They provide little support for or seem to have little relevance to the emphasis on man's limitations or on his potentialities—emphases that for earlier historians did have clear moral and ethical implications. Yet, this absence of *human nature* as an operant term does not mean that the emphasis on historical explanation in scientific terms leaves us on a bleak and hopeless plateau. Historical scholarship will doubtless continue to profit from the rich insights into human nature that the humanistic approach at its best has given us. But knowledge and understanding of a precise and verifiable sort may have its own moral and ethical implications. Insofar as the newer scientific tools advance historical knowledge about the particular situations and conditions that have guided, accentuated, or lessened man's limitations or that have fostered his potentialities, including his ethical potentialities, then historical inquiry and explanation of man's behavior in the past need not be regarded as the death-knell of ethical values; it may even add dimensions and components we have not thus far recognized.

NOTES TO CHAPTER I

[1]Arthur O. Lovejoy, *Reflections on Human Nature* (Baltimore, 1961) and Wilhelm Dilthey, *Gesammelte Schriften* (Leipzig, 1914-1931, 8 vols.). See Hajo Holborn, "Wilhelm Dilthey and the Critique of Historical Reason," *The Journal of the History of Ideas*, XI (1950), 93-118. Dilthey (1833-1911) was the founder of Lebensphilosophie. His conception of life makes unnecessary the distinction between intellect and reality and the corresponding dichotomy of spirit-matter. It sets up his system in opposition to the traditional Vernuftwissenschaft type of philosophy. In social science he is identified with Geistwissenschaft movements. He was concerned, not with social control, but with the conservation and objective revaluation of cultural forms.

[2]Especially noteworthy are Robert C. Binkley, "The Twentieth Century Looks at Human Nature," *Virginia Quarterly Review*, X (July, 1934), 336-50; and James Luther Adams, "The Changing Reputation of Human Nature," *The Journal of Liberal Religion*, IV (Autumn, 1942), 59-79. For Dewey's article, see *Encyclopedia of the Social Sciences* (New York, 1937), IV, 531-36.

[3]William Bradford, *A History of Plymouth Plantation* (Boston, 1901), 308 ff., 460.

[4]Bradford, 517-18.

[5]Bradford, 32.

[6]Thomas Hutchinson, *The History of the Colony and Province of Massachusetts-bay*, Lawrence Mayo, ed. (Cambridge, Mass., 1936, 3 vols.), II, 13 and 17-18.

[7]Hutchinson, II, 47.

[8]Hutchinson, I, 62-63.

[9]Hutchinson, II, 44.

[10]Hutchinson, II, 343.

[11]See my article, "Human Nature in American Thought: The Retreat from Reason in the Age of Science," in *Probing Our Past* (New York, 1955), 152-71.

[12]For many of these observations on Parkman, I am indebted to an article by my former student Richard Thompson, "Francis

Parkman on the Nature of Man," *Mid-America*, XLII (January, 1960), 3-18.

13Francis Parkman, "Our Best Classes and the National Politics," Boston *Daily Advertiser*, July 21, 1863; cited in Thompson's article.

14*The Jesuits in North America* (Boston and New York, 1903, 2 vols.), I, 21.

15William R. Taylor, "A Journey into the Human Mind: Motivation in Francis Parkman's *LaSalle*," *William and Mary Quarterly*, 3d ser., XIX (April, 1962), 220-37.

16*A History of the Expansion of Christianity* (New York, 1937-1945, 7 vols.).

17*Cf.* N. P. Jacobson, "Niebuhr's Philosophy of History," *Harvard Theological Review*, XXXVII, 4 (October, 1944), 237-68.

18Reinhold Niebuhr, *Man's Nature and Community* (New York, 1965); see especially 30, 70-75, 106-31.

19Niebuhr, *The Irony of American History* (New York, 1952); *Moral Man and Immoral Society* (New York, 1932, 1960); with Alan Heimert, *A Nation So Conceived* (New York, 1963); see also Page Smith, *The Historian and History* (New York, 1964), 75-76.

20*Moral Man and Immoral Society*, 2.

21Perry Miller, "Introduction," *The Puritans*, Miller and Thomas H. Johnson, eds. (New York, 1938, 1963, 2 vols.), I, 62-63.

22*The Vital Center* (Boston, 1949), 38-39.

23"The Causes of the Civil War: A Note on Historical Sentimentalism," *The Partisan Review*, XVI (1949), 969-81; reprinted in *American Historians: A Selection*, Harvey Wish, ed. (Oxford, 1962), 422-36, 435.

24David Noble, *The Paradox of Progressive Thought* (Minneapolis, 1958), 247; *cf.* Robert Allen Skotheim, "'Innocence' and 'Beyond Innocence' in Recent American Scholarship," *American Quarterly*, XIII (Spring, 1961), 93-99.

25Robert Osgood, *Ideals and Self-Interest in America's Foreign Relations* (Chicago, 1953), 430; cited in Skotheim, 97.

26May, *The End of American Innocence* (New York, 1959), 393; *cf.* Skotheim, 93.

27R. W. B. Lewis, *The American Adam: Innocence, Tragedy, and Tradition in the Nineteenth Century* (Chicago, 1955), 195.

NOTES TO CHAPTER II

[1]Adrienne Koch, ed., *The American Enlightenment* (New York, 1965), 19-48.

[2]*The Writings of Thomas Jefferson* (Monticello Edition, Washington, 1903-1905, 20 vols.), II, 165.

[3]*Writings,* XV, 274.

[4]*Writings,* II, 225.

[5]David Ramsay, *History of the American Revolution* (London, 1793, 2 vols.), I, 294. See also William Raymond Smith, *History As Argument: Three Patriot Histories of the American Revolution* (The Hague, 1966), espec. 40-72.

[6]*Reflections,* 87.

[7]Ramsay, I, 333, 338.

[8]Ramsay, I, 348.

[9]Ramsay, I, 29.

[10]Ramsay, I, 33.

[11]Ramsay, II, 315-25, 354-56.

[12]Mercy Warren, *The Rise, Progress, and Termination of the American Revolution* (Boston, 1805, 2 vols.), I, 2.

[13]Warren, I, 5.

[14]Warren, I, 20; see also 16-19.

[15]Warren, I, vii.

[16]*Collections of the Massachusetts Historical Society,* 5th ser., IV, 502 ff.

[17]For an account of Williams, see Ralph N. Miller, "Samuel Williams' 'History of Vermont,'" *New England Quarterly,* XXII (March, 1949), 73-84.

[18]Williams, *The Natural and Civil History of Vermont* (Walpole, N. H., 1794), I, ix ff, 250.

[19]Williams, *History,* I, xi, and II, 266-67.

[20]Williams, *History,* I, xi, and *passim.*

[21]Williams, *History,* I, 158-59.

[22]Williams, *History,* I, ix.

[23]In addition to the biographies, especially Russell Nye, *George Bancroft, Brahmin Rebel* (New York, 1944), I am indebted to an essay by a former student, John W. Rathbun, "George Bancroft on

NOTES **113**

Man and History," *Wisconsin Academy of Sciences, Arts and Letters,* XLIII (September, 1954), 51-72.

24Bancroft, *Literary and Historical Miscellanies* (New York, 1855), 33 ff.

25Bancroft's explicit discussions of his theory of human nature can be understood from his addresses, "The Office of the People in Art, Government, and Religion" (1835), "On the Progress of Civilization" (1838), and "The Progress of Mankind" (1854), all in *Literary and Historical Miscellanies.*

26For examples, see *History of the United States from the Discovery of the Continent* (London, 1852, 6 vols.), I, 4, 7, 404, and III, 188. See also the Author's Last Edition (New York, 1896-1897, 6 vols.), II, 125-29, 136, 324-34, and VI, 442-45, 451, 474. For a discriminating comment on some of the differences in emphasis between the earlier and the post-Civil War editions, see *North American Review,* CXX (1875), 424 ff.

27The literature on Turner is too considerable to give even a selective sample. See Merle Curti, "The Section and Frontier in American History: The Methodological Concepts of Frederick Jackson Turner," in Stuart Rice, ed., *Methods in Social Science: A Case Book* (Chicago, 1931), 353-67, and "Frederick Jackson Turner, 1861-1932," in *Probing Our Past* (New York, 1955), 32-55. Especially important are the contributions of Dr. Fulmer Mood to Turner scholarship of which "Turner's Formative Period," in *The Early Writings of Frederick Jackson Turner* (Madison, Wisconsin, 1938) is a notable early example.

28See especially Harry Elmer Barnes, *The New History and the Social Studies* (New York, 1925), James Harvey Robinson, *The New History* (New York, 1912), and Donald M. Scott, "Generous Souls Amid Catastrophes: Charles Beard, James Harvey Robinson, Carl Becker," (University of Wisconsin, A Master's Essay, 1964).

29John Higham, "Intellectual History and Its Neighbors," *Journal of the History of Ideas,* XV, 3 (June, 1954), 339-47, 342.

30Beard review of N. J. Lennes, *Whither Democracy* (New York, 1927), in *New Republic,* LI (1927), 314-15.

31Perhaps Beard's views on human nature are best reflected in *The Republic* (New York, 1946), *passim.*

[32]Robert A. Skotheim, *American Intellectual Histories and Historians* (Princeton, 1966), 95-98, 100-103, 105-8.

[33]Beard, *The Nature of the Social Sciences* (New York, 1934), 60.

[34]Sidney Ratner, "The Historian's Approach to Psychology," *Journal of the History of Ideas*, II (January, 1941), 104.

[35]Kenneth Stampp, *The Peculiar Institution* (New York, 1956), vii.

[36]Stanley Elkins, *Slavery* (New York, 1963), 103-15.

[37]Herbert Aptheker, *American Negro Slave Revolts* (New York, 1943).

NOTES TO CHAPTER III

[1]Several secondary works have proved useful, especially Ernest Samuels, *Henry Adams: The Middle Years* (Cambridge, 1958), Elizabeth Stevenson, *A Biography of Henry Adams* (New York, 1955), Henry Wasser, *The Scientific Thought of Henry Adams* (Thessalonica, 1956), Max L. Baym, *The French Education of Henry Adams* (New York, 1951), and William B. Jordy, *Henry Adams, Scientific Historian* (New Haven, 1952).

[2]Worthington C. Ford, ed., *Letters of Henry Adams* (Boston, 1930), I, 206.

[3]*Letters*, II, 235-37.

[4]*Letters*, II, 235-37.

[5]Wasser, 116-17; Max L. Baym, "William James and Henry Adams," *New England Quarterly*, X (December, 1937), 717-42; *The Education of Henry Adams* (New York, 1946), 231.

[6]*North American Review*, CXIV (April, 1872), 435-40.

[7]Harold Dan Cater, ed., *Henry Adams and His Friends* (Boston, 1947), 121-22.

[8]*North American Review*, CXX (April, 1875), 424-37.

[9]Adams, *History of the United States* (New York, 1930), I, 159-60; *Life of Albert Gallatin* (Philadelphia, 1880), 171.

[10]*History*, I, 334, IX, 226.

[11]*History*, VII, 97.

[12]*History*, IV, 276 ff.

[13]*History*, VI, 403.

[14]*History*, I, 172, II, 34, V, 54, and *North American Review*, CXXIII (October, 1876), 331.

[15]*Gallatin*, 171.

[16]*North American Review*, CXXII (April, 1876), 361.

[17]*History*, IX, 240.

[18]*History*, I, 159-60, IX, 220.

[19]*History*, I, 106-7.

[20]*Education*, 231; *Letters*, II, 235-37.

[21]See, for analysis and criticisms: Jordy and Wasser, *passim*.

[22]Harry Elmer Barnes, *History and Social Intelligence* (New York, 1926), 525 and 552; and William Langer, "The Next Assignment," *The American Historical Review*, LXII (1958), 283-304.

[23]The more important discussions include Sidney Ratner, "The Historian's Approach to Psychology," *Journal of the History of Ideas*, II (January, 1941), 95-109; Edward Saveth, "The Historian and the Freudian Approach to History," *New York Times Book Review*, January 1, 1956, 7-8; Hans Meyerhoff, "On Psychoanalysis and History," *Psychoanalysis and the Psychoanalytic Review*, XLIX (1962), 18-19; Bruce Mazlish, ed., *Psychoanalysis and History* (Englewood Cliffs, New Jersey, 1963); John Burnham's review of Norman O. Brown, *Life Against Death* (Middletown, Conn., 1959); Erik Erikson, *Young Man Luther* (New York, 1958); and A. Bronson Feldman, *The Unconscious in History* (New York, 1959), in *Literature and Psychology*, XC (1960), 28-31.

[24]Dixon Wecter, *The Hero in America* (New York, 1941), 41 ff.

[25]David Brion Davis, "Some Themes of Counter Subversion," *Mississippi Valley Historical Review*, XLVII (September, 1960), 205-24.

[26]Stanley Elkins, *Slavery* (Chicago, 1959).

[27]Earl E. Thorpe, *Eros and Freedom in Southern Life and Thought* (Durham, 1967), *passim*.

[28]Preserved Smith, "Luther's Early Development in the Light of Psychoanalysis," *American Journal of Psychology*, XXIV (1913), 360-61; see also John A. Garraty, "Preserved Smith, Ralph V. Harlow, and Psychology," *Journal of the History of Ideas*, XV (June, 1954), 456-65.

[29]Erikson, *Young Man Luther* (New York, 1958).

[30]Ralph V. Harlow, *Samuel Adams* (New York, 1923), and again, Garraty, *loc. cit.*

[31]Two studies offer interesting comparisons: Alexander L. and Juliette L. George, *Woodrow Wilson and Colonel House: A Personality Study* (New York, 1956), and William C. Bullitt and Sigmund Freud, *Thomas Woodrow Wilson* (Boston, 1967).

[32]Fawn Brodie, *Thaddeus Stevens: Scourge of the South* (New York, 1959).

[33]David Donald, *Charles Sumner and the Coming of the Civil War* (New York, 1964).

[34]Emery Battis, *Saints and Sectaries: Anne Hutchinson and the Antinomian Controversy* (Chapel Hill, 1962).

[35]Richard L. Bushman, "On the Uses of Psychology: Conflict

and Conciliation in Benjamin Franklin," *History and Theory,* V (1966), 225-40.

[36]Dr. Frederick Wyatt and William B. Willcox, "Sir Henry Clinton: A Psychological Exploration," *William and Mary Quarterly,* XVI (1959), 3-26.

[37]Wyatt and Willcox; see also Willcox's *Portrait of a General* (New York, 1964).

[38]Lee Benson, *The Concept of Jacksonian Democracy* (New York, 1964), VII, 329.

[39]Stephan Thernstrom, *Poverty and Progress: Social Mobility in a Nineteenth Century City* (Cambridge, Mass., 1964).

[40]Lee Benson and Cushing Strout, "Causation and the American Civil War: Two Appraisals," *History and Theory,* I (1961), 162-73.

[41]Thomas C. Cochran, "A Model for Cultural Factors," in *The Inner Revolution* (New York, 1964), 128 ff.

[42]Robert W. Doherty, "Status Anxiety and American Reform: Some Alternatives," *American Quarterly,* XIX, 2 (Summer, 1967), 329-33.

Afterword

MERLE CURTI's *Human Nature in American Historical Thought* was originally presented at the University of Missouri in the form of three public lectures on March 13 and 14, 1968, the seventh of the Paul Anthony Brick Lectures, a series of commentaries on various aspects of the "science of ethics" made possible by the bequest of Paul Anthony Brick, a citizen of Missouri at the time of his death.

The first Brick Lectures, *Morals for Mankind,* were delivered in 1960 by Herbert W. Schneider, professor emeritus of philosophy at Columbia University, and published by the University of Missouri Press the following year. Subsequent titles in the series, all of them similarly published, are *The Three Worlds of Man,* 1962, by Stringfellow Barr, educator, author, and editor; *The Reluctant Revolutionary,* 1963, by Edward Teller, physicist and recipient of the Albert Einstein Medal for 1959; *The Ethics of United States Foreign Relations,* 1964, by Erwin D. Canham, editor-in-chief of *The Christian Science Monitor; The Man in the Middle,* 1965, by Harry S. Ashmore, recipient of the Pulitzer Prize in Journalism for 1958 as editor of the Little Rock *Arkansas Gazette,* which was also awarded a Pulitzer Prize; and *The Persistent Quest for Values: What Are We Seeking?* 1966, by Harlan Hatcher, president of The University of Michigan.

WILLIAM PEDEN
Chairman, Brick Committee